NARMER

NARMER

By

Kesnor C. Williams

Seshat Djehuti Inc.   Cheyenne, Wyoming

Seshat Djehuti Inc.

Cheyenne, Wyoming

Copyright 2017 by Kesnor Williams

Printed in the United States of America

ISBN: **978-0-9995402-3-7**

CONTENTS

Dedication

To the timeless Creator energies, which continues to resurrect and create history that stands the test of time.

Foreword

Over the years one of the most frequent questions I would get asked by anyone who knew of this project was, why would I choose to do a period piece when a modern day story about anything else would be so much easier, requiring less research. I would always avoid answering those types of questions to keep myself from being deterred. So to all whom I didn't answer, and to whom ever else that may be curious as to why I would chose to do a period piece like Narmer instead of a modern day story. There were several different factors, which inspired me to write this Novel. The main one is the passion that I have for stories of this genre. I could remember growing up watching and admiring movies like Gladiator, Shaka Zulu, Troy, Alexander, Kingdom of Heaven, and dreaming that one-day I would be able to be a part of creating a project of that magnitude. And when I say a project of that magnitude, I specifically mean for both its cultural and its historical references. To be able to draw from a specific time in history, and make it relevant and acceptable in modern time by way of literature or the Hollywood culture, has always been a dream of mine.

Another factor that inspired me to write this Novel was because of how historically significant I considered the main character Narmer aka Menes to be. Even though it is another period piece based off of recorded history, it is very different from the movies that I grew up watching and admiring. Even very different from Shaka Zulu, though they both share the very obvious similarity of Africans being some of the most essential characters in the story. I must say there similarity does not go much further than that. Narmer separates itself from the pack by taking you back to 3100 B.C. A time when the continent of Africa was the influence and inspiration to the rest of the world, due to the Kushite Empire's highly advanced Nile Valley Civilization.

This fact was very instrumental in me writing this story. The fact that never before, or at least not to my knowledge has the history of Narmer aka Menes and how the Nile Valley Civilization enlightened, and spear headed the growth of the rest of the world, been used as the focal point of any Novel, Screenplay or movie etc. So for me a history buff and an aspiring screenplay writer, I was very excited and felt very lucky to find such a significant story in world history that was practically untouched in the world of entertainment. I just hope and wish that when this body of work is presented to the world as a whole, that this work is loved by all fans of history, literature, theater, and cinema, or at the very least respected. I truly hope so, because as an artist what more could one ask for.

By Kesnor C. Williams

Preface

Narmer is a thrilling, action packed, fictionalized screenplay based on the historical achievement of the Kushite leader and King of Kings Narmer aka Menes, a reluctant leader who is chosen to be King after he leads his Empire in war against foreign invaders trying to usurp power.

Dated back to 3100 B.C. this story details Narmer's rise from the Chief of a small village to becoming King of the Kushite Empire, and starting the African dynastic lineage. A dynastic lineage which today historical, and archaeological evidence show us that they were the leaders of one of the most highly advanced civilization of that time.

Narmer takes you back to a time when Africa and its Nile Valley Civilization were the influence, and breadbasket to the known world. They projected endless prosperity because of their strong food production, thanks to the rich soil courtesy of the yearly floods of the overflowing Nile River. Combined with the Kushite people's highly advanced concepts of science, technology, and spirituality. The people in the Nile Valley of Northeast Africa achieved heights that amazed visitors from foreign lands.

This lead neighboring countries, who were familiar with the Nile Valley's prosperity to naturally want a piece of this world famous breadbasket. So in their pursuit for a stronger economy, and world recognition, the natives of these neighboring countries continually migrated to the Nile Valley with dreams of wealth and power. The foreigners arrived as traders whom operated on the Mediterranean seacoast, but eventually they evolved into several different prosperous communities within the Delta regions. An area, which the Kushites simultaneously use as a welcoming area to play host to the rest of the world, while displaying the heights of their Nile Valley civilization and their Kushite Empire.

Even though the Delta is a part of the Kushite Empire, because of the difference in altitude above sea level and the steady increase of foreign settlers. The Kushites viewed it as a separate region, and ruled from their throne farther south at Thebes. The authority of the throne being in the south at Thebes only lead to more and more foreigners landing in the Delta region to call the Nile Valley their home. This practice eventually frustrated the Kushites. So after continuous warnings to the foreigners, to stop the migrating of their countrymen into the Delta regions and the foreign population failing to do so. Narmer and the rest of the Kushite Empire rage war against the foreigners, and take back full control of the Delta regions. Once again unifying the upper and lower regions of the Kushite Empire as one.

By Kesnor C. Williams

FADE IN:

3100 B.C. NILE VALLEY DELTA OF NORTHEAST AFRICA

EXT. NILE VALLEY AFRICA - NIGHT

A normal night, an ASWAN WARRIOR creeps through some bushes with a spear in his hand. He sneaks towards the Mumon village. He reaches a lookout peek that overlooks lower Kush, the lower Delta regions, and the Mediterranean Sea.

Something catches the warrior's attention, and distracts him. He turns to get a better look.

He notices three boats come shore, and dock in the already overcrowded Delta. The Aswan warrior lets his guard down for a moment, and a spear hits him in the back. He falls to the ground, and die.

                    ASWAN WARRIOR
               (gets hit)
          Aah!

The MUMON KILLER walks over to the Aswan warrior's dead body, takes out the spear, and stabs him again to make sure he's dead.

The Mumon Killer lets out a loud warrior's cry.

                    MUMON KILLER
          Yee ye ya ya ya!

The Mumon killer's UNIT appears behind him. They continue moving forward together but only for a few yards. They walk into an all out assault by the Aswan warriors.

A war begins. Arrows fly, spears are thrown, and swords slash. As the hand-to-hand combat becomes more deadly, DUBA, the Aswan Chief, unleashes his dominance and superiority on the battlefield.

EXT. DOCKS OF THE NILE VALLEY DELTA - NIGHT

JAUGEN walks behind BEN.

                    JAUGEN
          Are you sure this is the boat that they are
          supposed to be on?

                    BEN
                (upset)
        For the hundredth time, yes the bloody
        voyager. Now stop badgering me, and
        keep an eye out for them.

ALSI shouts from the boat.

                    ALSI
        Ben the great traveler, traveling to
        wherever the next adventure might take
        him.

                    BEN
                (shouts back)
        Alsi, the sliest of all foxes, so natives
        guard your pots.

Ben and Alsi walk toward each other, shake hands and hug.

                    BEN
        Alsi, it is good to see you again. Welcome
        to the Nile Valley and it's ancient Nowe
        Taseti.

                    ALSI
        Likewise, it is good seeing you again
        cousin. It has been too long.

                    BEN
        Longer than I wish to believe, but the Nile
        Valley is not a place that one visits and
        leaves quickly. It's the contrary, it's a place
        with so much beauty, prosperity, and life's
        pleasures that one lifetime is not enough
        to experience it all. So men often come
        here and get lost in time.

                    ALSI
        So I have heard. The pleasures and beauty
        of the Nile Valley, and their advance
        civilization are sung all throughout our
        country. From North, South, East to West.

                    BEN
        I will assure you that the most alluring tale
        that you have heard will be a hundred
        folds better when experienced in person.

                    ALSI
        Experiencing even a pinch of what I have
        heard will eclipse all my life's expectancy.

Alsi notices Jaugen.

                    ALSI
        Is that? It is. Jaugen of the Preston family.

Alsi greets Jaugen.

                    ALSI
        Well this is certainly a pleasant surprise
        old friend. I didn't expect to see you here.

                    JAUGEN
        Nor did I old friend, but life is unpredictable
        like this sometimes.

                    ALSI
        It clearly seems that life is.

Alsi is surprised to see Ben and Jaugen together. He introduces his companion.

                    ALSI
        Ben, you remember my son Srtife?

Ben shakes SRTIFE's hand.

                    BEN
        This is your firstborn son Srtife? It seems
        as if you have grown into a man overnight.

                    SRTIFE
        A man and ready for the world, sir.

                    BEN
        Oh, it is so refreshing to see fellow
        countrymen who are young, anxious and
        full of ambition. Seeing you brings back
        memories of my sons back in the old

country, Kevin and Omar. You were all
children playing on the hillside when I
left. Are they still your companions?

                    SRTIFE
Yes they are sir, two of my dearest friends,
and they both think and speak the world of
you their father.

                    BEN
            (proudly)
Do they? If only I had known that they
have grown to be young adventurers such
as your-self, I would have requested them
also. I must see to it that I do so, now
seeing that you their companion are ready
for the adventure of the world.

                    ALSI
I assure you cousin. You would be very
proud of your sons, and the new seeds of
fruits and vegetables you have sent for
them, have made them quite the
agriculturalists.

                    BEN
Really now. Let us go and have a drink, and
catch up on old times.
            (to Jaugen)
Jaugen, grab their loads and come along.

                    ALSI
That is not necessary. We are capable of
carrying our own load.

                    BEN
Nonsense. That is why he is here.

Jaugen picks up the luggage. Jaugen despises the conditions he is obligated to.

                    ALSI
            (surprised)
And life just keeps getting more and more
unpredictable.

                    (to Alsi)
          Come along old friend. So how is my father
          doing?

                         ALSI
          He sends his best wishes, and declares
          how proud he is to be your father.

INT. NARMER PALACE - NIGHT

Further South at Nekheb. CHIEF NARMER meditates at his palace. He prays.

                    CHIEF NARMER
          Almighty Creator thanks and praises to
          you for seeing me through all the days of
          my life. Thanks to all the Ntchru for
          guiding and protecting me through all of
          my doings. Honor and praises to our
          forefathers who have came before us and
          showed us the way. Your principles will be
          magnified.

EXT. NARMER PALACE - NIGHT

FUSA, Narmer's General of the Nekheb warriors, walks up and addresses Narmer's personal GUARDS.

                         FUSA
          I must speak with the chief at once.

                     N GUARD 1
          The Chief is conversing with the Ntchru
          and wishes not to be disturbed.

                         FUSA
          This matter is most urgent. I must speak
          to him at once.

Fusa attempts to walk past. The Guards stop him.

                     N GUARD 2
          My apologies General Fusa, but the Chief
          commanded us not to let anyone enter
          these doors.

The Guard holds back General Fusa with a hand on his chest.

>   FUSA
>   If you wish to use that hand again you will
>   remove it.

INT. NARMER PALACE - NIGHT

Chief Narmer walks to the door to calm down the commotion.

EXT. NARMER PALACE - NIGHT

>   N GUARD 1
>   It's just... well... You know the wrath of the
>   Chief, when his orders are not followed.

>   FUSA
>   What part of it is urgent, do you not
>   understand?

Fusa pushes the guards out of his way as Chief Narmer opens the door.

>   CHIEF NARMER
>   At ease men.

The guards bow and steps aside.

>   CHIEF NARMER
>   General Fusa. Greetings warrior.

>   FUSA
>   Hail the Chief.

>   CHIEF NARMER
>   Please do come in.

>   FUSA
>   Thank you Chief.

They walk inside.

                    FUSA
I came to notify you that the Foreigners
have just docked three more boats in the
Delta.

                    CHIEF NARMER
This ongoing entry of these Foreigners
into our native land will be the death of
our nation. They have no intentions on
living up to their agreement. Between
them and the foreigners with the
caravans from the Far East this is now the
third landing since the summer solstice.

                    FUSA
So what do you suppose we do about it?

                    CHIEF NARMER
We must start making our presence and
intentions felt in the Delta regions. Start
governing and patrolling the seacoast like
we use to, and turn the Delta back into our
native Taseti.

                    FUSA
But our great grandfather Sakmra gave the
foreigners permission to live in the Delta
as freemen. Welcome by us as long as they
do not cross the borders at Athra.

                    CHIEF NARMER
Yes, but they were also to live in
compliance with the Empire, and with the
treaty stating no more smuggling in of
their people into our country. Let us not
forget that it was their steadfast
migrating to our country, which led to the
borders being created by Sakmra in the
first place. Foreigners so populated our
land then, to stay connected to the Ntchru
we had to move our throne south to
Thebes, away from some of our most
fertile soil. But as usual the foreign
population is never content, as soon as

they saw weakness in the local
leadership, they raged war for more land
and trade routes. I refuse to sit and let the
same pattern repeat itself.

                    FUSA
But we cannot just force them out. We
must first consult with the King and the
other members of the council, to get the
blessing of the council.

                CHIEF NARMER
And what about you my flesh and blood,
my general, my dearest friend, do I have
your blessing?

                    FUSA
Narmer you are my cousin, my dearest
friend since childhood, and the Chief of our
people whom have the highest of respect
for you. I will stand by any decision with
you.

                CHIEF NARMER
          (reaffirms)
And with you Fusa, I will take on any
opposition.

                    FUSA
So then, I will have messages sent to all the
Chiefs, Elders, and Temple Keepers of the
other villages. Requesting a meeting at the
Nekheb hall 15 days from today.

                CHIEF NARMER
Yes, and invite them all to come and eat
breakfast, at the Nekheb dining hall before
the meeting. But make it 20 days from
today, to give our brothers at Meroe and
Kuru sufficient time to get here. As for the
King, I will go and see him personally. It is
about time that I go and pay my respect
anyway. My visit is well past due.

                    FUSA
          I will take care of it my Chief. And what am
          I to tell the council, is the reason as to why
          you are requesting this meeting, because
          we both know that all of the council
          members do not disagree with the
          landings of the foreigners and are liable to
          not attend.

                 CHIEF NARMER
          I know. Tell them it is to put an end to the
          confusion between our brothers the
          Aswans and the Mumons. Both of whom I
          want you to go and see personally. Tell
          them this ongoing feud must stop, and
          they are both to report to the meeting of
          the council. At which time the Empire will
          once and for all, come up with a solution
          that they both will respect and live by.

                    FUSA
          I will take care of it my Chief.

Fusa and Chief Narmer exchange respectful bows, then go their separate ways.

EXT. MUMON VILLAGAE - ASWANS AND MUMONS WAR - NIGHT

In the middle of the war between the Awans and the Mumons, The Aswan Chief,
DUBA, is ferocious. He slays every opposition in his way. Duba leads his WARRIORS
to victory and overtakes the Mumon's village.

The Aswan's sound a DRUM in victory as Duba lifts his spear in the air and lets out a
victory yell with his warriors.

                    DUBA
          Aha!

                 ASWAN WARRIORS
          Aha!

INT. NARMER'S PALACE - NIGHT

Chief Narmer recognizes the SOUND OF THE DRUM and walks out onto his balcony.
He looks into the distance, towards the Nile River and the Mumon's village. Orange
flames blaze in the darkness. Smoke rises into the air.

A CAT jumps up onto the balcony and meows at Chief Narmer, which gets his attention. He grabs a pitcher of milk, and pours some for the cat. The cat drinks it.

Chief Narmer stands back up, and gaze at the flames in the distance.

                    CHIEF NARMER
          This meeting is more necessary than I
          thought.

INT. BAR - NIGHT

                    ALSI
          Really. I had no idea you were married
          with four children.

                    BEN
          That's right, two wives and four children.

                    ALSI
          Two wives! How did you ever manage to
          pull that one off?

                    JAUGEN
               (laughs)
          Easy, just be able to afford it.

                    SRTIFE
          Two wives, that doesn't sound bad at all.

Srtife knocks his mug together with Jaugen in a toast.

                    BEN
          Actually this is one of my favorite Kushite
          customs, because it allows me to have
          more than one wife.

                    ALSI
          And the Kushites do not mind foreign
          men taking their women as wives?

                    BEN
          Sure they mind, but there are ways of
          getting around their resentments. Ways
          to even make them accept it and
          recognize it as a legal marriage. There are
          a lot of men-

                    JAUGEN
What is that?

                    BEN
What is what?

                    JAUGEN
Do you hear that?

                    ALSI
I hear it. It sounds like some kind of
drumming. What is that?

                    JAUGEN
              (gets excited)
The sweet sound of me collecting my
winnings old friend. That's right you saps,
pay up. You hear the sweet drumming of
my victory, that's right, pay up.

Jaugen stands and walks around the room, to collect his winnings.

                    JAUGEN
That's right. Give it here.

Jaugen collects from one MAN and turns to ANOTHER.

                    JAUGEN
You too, Laoi, my ugly Far East friend. Pay
up.

LAOI hands his payment over to Jaugen.

                    LAOI
Fast Jaugen you are one lucky foreign
bastard. One of these days your luck is
going to run out, and I will be there to
bask in the occasion.

                    JAUGEN
Is that right my friend, well I will see you
there, when that day comes.

Jaugen turns to see who else in the room owes him.

                    JAUGEN
        Jugo my bread and meat, what do you
        have prepared for me to eat?

JUGO pays Jaugen and says to him.

                    JUGO
        Die slow from an infested blade you
        human waste.

                    JAUGEN
                 (sarcastically)
        Aaaah! Jugo I love you too. I swear I do.

Jaugen continues to collect from everyone in the room that owes him. Jaugen spots Babu.

                    JAUGEN
        Babu, just the man I need to see.

Jaugen walks over to Babu.

Meanwhile across the bar, Alsi says to Ben.

                    ALSI
        I see fast Jaugen Preston is still a betting
        man. What is all that about?

                    BEN
        That drumming you hear is a signal
        indicating that one village has just
        conquered another. Most likely it is
        between the Mumons and the Aswans, the
        aftermath of three young women being
        kidnapped last week. There was an
        ongoing bet to see how long it would take
        before there was a retaliation. And as you
        can see fast Jaugen Preston won the bet.
        But to the foreign population of the Delta
        goes the spoil. Because when the Kushites
        fight amongst themselves, they are too
        preoccupied to pay attention to anything
        else that is going on. And believe you me
        the Kushites are always fighting against
        each other. It is unexplainable, even with
        all their breath taking achievements, and

their advance way of life, they just cannot
seem to get past killing each other.

Alsi grabs his mug and raises it.

                    ALSI
Well then let us all drink to opportunity.

They knock their mugs together in a toast and take a sip.

                    ALSI
I am impressed to see that the two of you
my fellow countrymen have learned so
much about the Kushites, that you all are
able to predict their next move.

                    BEN
Well learning the ways of the Kushites is
easier than you might think. When
dealing with them there are two basic
things one must remember. First is
anything that is permitted by them is
practiced by them everyday through their
daily living. It is a sight to see. At times
they all seem to be working off of one
common thought, inspired by their
Ntchru and their Ancestors. Whom all of
them seems to consult with for answers
and directions in life on a daily basis.

                    ALSI
I know what an ancestor is, but whom or
what is a Ntchru?

                    BEN
The ones they say is responsible for them
having life, the ones responsible for
everything that exists. The uncreated
creators, it is a cultural phenomenon
here. They sacrifice their lives to them.
Build monuments dedicated to them
specifically for worshiping. I think it is
this common bond, which propels them to
excel in their understanding of nature, in
their trading with neighboring villages, in
their brick masonry, pottery making, arts

and crafts, boat making, and so forth. I think this common bond is their greatest achievement, because it compels them to unite and achieve.

                    ALSI
This is quite fascinating. I must learn more about these Ntchru. What is the other?

                    BEN
What is the other what?

                    ALSI
You said there were two things to remember when dealing with the Kushites. What is the other?

                    BEN
Oh, it is the most important thing of all, anyone or anything that offends them, or their way of life will surely be killed. Or if they are lucky, get taken as a prisoner, and sold as a slave. That is how I ran into our old friend over there.

Ben points at Jaugen.

                    ALSI
What do you mean?

                    BEN
I bought him as a slave, at a town auction. I recognized who he was, and purchased him.

                    ALSI
Oh! That explains the bag carrying and so forth. What did he do to become a prisoner for sale?

                    BEN
He lived further south at Semna in the more native populated area, where he became a fairly successful goldsmith. Jaugen made a good life for himself, four wives and numerous children.

Unfortunately for him, he got drunk one
night, and urinated on one of the temples
dedicated to HAPI the Kushites Ntchr for
water. If Jaugen was not a well-known
goldsmith in the village, they would have
killed him for sure, but the respected
members of the foreign community
pleaded for him, so the Kushites
pardoned him from the spear, and instead
sold him as a slave. Jaugen truly has luck
on his side, because without a doubt for
an offense like that, these Kushites will
surely have your head.

                    ALSI
                 (curiously)
Exactly how violent are the natives?

                    BEN
You will find for the most part, they are all
very easy going, until you have offended
them.

Jaugen tries to bargain with Babu.

                    BABU
No deal. You never pay on time. You still
owe me for the horse I gave you three
harvest ago. Fast Jaugen, you are bad for
business, everyone knows that.

                    JAUGEN
I cannot believe that this is what our
relationship has come to.

Jaugen takes out the payment to pay, and bribe Babu.

                    JAUGEN
I am telling you that I wish to finish
paying you for the horse now, and also
put a down payment on you finding me a
woman. She doesn't even have to be
pretty or young, just someone to pass the
time. Huh, How about it?

Babu takes what he is owed and leaves the rest.

BABU
Nothing has changed, still no deal.

JAUGEN
Oh come on. I told you my wife is
pregnant, it's not my fault Kushite
customs forbid me to copulate with her
for the duration of her pregnancy. What
am I suppose to do?

BABU
Either you find someone else to sell you a
woman for half price, or you can get a
wife like any self respecting man would.
By her actually being attracted to you!

JAUGEN
I cannot believe this is how you are dealing
with me. In Semna, did I not often give you
extra gold when we traded?

BABU
That was to bribe the Nomadic tribes in
the area for you.

JAUGEN
How about when I got your nephew work
in the mines? I took him from cattle
herding to being a goldsmith.

BABU
Haa! What goldsmith? You had him in the
mines digging, doing slave labor.

JAUGEN
He had to start from somewhere.

Srtife walks over to Jaugen's table.

SRTIFE
Ben says it is time to leave, before the
natives come investigating the landings.

Jaugen nods.

                    JAUGEN
So how about it, at least tell me if you
come across any extras you will keep me
in mind.

                    BABU
I have no reason to make promises to you.
I will assure you just as I assure all my
customers, when you meet my price, you
will have your merchandise.

Jaugen leaves with his bribe.

EXT. BAR - DAY

Srtife walks out into the sunlight. He takes a deep breath to savor the moment.

                    SRTIFE
Ah, my first sunrise in Kush. Life is truly
amazing, just two weeks ago I could only
dream of being here. Now here I stand in
the Nile Valley, the land of opportunity.

Srtife spreads his arms and spins around, as he takes in the view and shouts.

                    SRTIFE
Anxious for whatever opportunity awaits
me.

Alsi and Ben notice Srtife, as they gather their horses.

                    BEN
Do you think we were ever that tenacious,
when we were his age?

                    ALSI
I am too old to remember, but not too old
to learn. For the past couple of years it has
been Srtife, whom I have been gathering
my inspiration and strength from.

                    BEN
Oh, to be young and inspired is one of the
greatest feelings in life. If only man could
harvest it and sell it in the market.

Jaugen walks out of the bar and catches up.

> ALSI
> Everyone regardless of age or stature in
> life would consume it.

Alsi notices that Srtife is too caught up in the moment.

> ALSI
> (to Srtife)
> Okay son, gather yourself and let us be on
> our way. It is an entire day's ride to reach
> our destination.

Srtife walks over and mounts his horse.

> BEN
> Pace yourself son. There will be lots to see
> along the journey that will amaze you.

> SRTIFE
> I truly hope so.

They start the ride.

> SRTIFE
> It is an entire day's ride to your home you
> say?

> BEN
> Yes, one whole day. Give or take a little.

> SRTIFE
> What village do you live in?

> BEN
> The village of Buba.

> SRTIFE
> Tell me. Are there many beautiful women
> in Buba?

INT. KINGS'S PALACE IN THEBES - DAY

KING SALO is in his study when the KING's GUARD approaches to notify him.

                    KING'S GUARD
Pardon me my King.

                    KING SALO
Yes, what is it?

                    KING'S GUARD
Chief Narmer is on his way up to see you.

King Solo anxiously puts down his pen and goes to greet Narmer. He stands atop his palace steps and watches Narmer ride up, give the handler his horse, and enter the stairway.

                    CHIEF NARMER
          (kneels)
Greetings my king.

                    KING SALO
Chief Narmer, welcome to my palace once
again. It has been too long.

                    CHIEF NARMER
          (stands)
My king it is always an honor to be in your
presence.

                    KING SALO
The honor is mine young chief. I am not
blessed with your company often enough.
How is your chief wife and children?

                    CHIEF NARMER
Thank you for asking, they are all doing
well. Berenib sends her love.

                    KING SALO
The ever-lovely Berenib, as glorious as a
flower bathing in Atun's rays.

They walk.

                    KING SALO
She shows so much pride, I would not
doubt that she by herself could lead a
nation. You could not have made a better

choice in choosing a chief wife. I trust you
are doing right by her.

                    CHIEF NARMER
          She would have it no other way. And how
          is the queen?

                    KING SALO
          She is good, as healthy as ever still
          standing by my side.

                    CHIEF NARMER
          That is wonderful. And how about you,
          how are you feeling these days?

                    KING SALO
          My day is coming.

King Salo gets to the point.

                    KING SALO
          But I know you did not come here to talk
          about an old man's health. Whenever I get
          a personal visit from you, more than likely
          you have an issue to address.

They walk into the study.

                    CHIEF NARMER
          My king, you know me all too well.

                    KING SALO
              (proudly)
          Please, take a seat.

                    CHIEF NARMER
          Yes, thank you.

                    KING SALO
          Would you like some refreshments?

                    CHIEF NARMER
          Yes my King, thank you.

The King and Narmer take a few grapes from a fruit bowl to eat while they talk.

                    KING SALO
So what is it that has brought you here to
Thebes?

                   CHIEF NARMER
I know that you are well aware of the
ongoing feud between the Aswans and the
Mumons.

The King fells bothered by the statement paces around the room. The statement
forces him to deal with the issue.

                   CHIEF NARMER
No disrespect, but I was wondering what
does the throne intend to do about it.
Because as we all heard last night, it is
now far beyond a simple quarrel with one
or two lives being lost.

                    KING SALO
Everyone in the Empire is aware of what
is going on, but what else am I to do? I
have addressed every member of the
council including you about this matter.
But in these times, the majority of Chiefs
are only concerned with issues that
threaten or benefit their own village.

Chief Narmer gets up to speak.

                   CHIEF NARMER
You are the appointed King of the Empire.
Sure you do not solely make decisions,
but you are the King. It is your duty to
assure justice and equality to every man
woman and child of every village.

                    KING SALO
I ruled along with the rest of the council
in our unanimous decision. Our decision
for both villages to divide the land
accordingly between themselves, and
respect the given borders. I left it up to
them to resolve their conflict them-selves.

CHIEF NARMER
(dissatisfied)
You expected them to resolve it themselves,
just by us indicating a respected border.
What happened to over seeing them, to
make sure that they both respect and
follow through with the council's ruling?

KING SALO
(looks at Narmer serious)
Yes, I could have done more, but more
initiative has to be taken by another
member of the council and the Chiefs.
(beat)
I am an old man. When it is not I, who will
it be?

CHIEF NARMER
I don't believe this, are we back on this
again?

KING SALO
Young ruler we never left.

CHIEF NARMER
You must pardon me my King if I don't see
why you naming your successor, should
prevent you from carrying out your Kingly
duties.

KING SALO
Like the majority of the members of the
council, I too was too preoccupied to keep
up with feuding neighbors. I have been in
Abydos and in the city of the dead, steadfast
finishing the third chamber on my tomb.
Besides everything was in order, up until a
week ago. Who could have predicted there
would have been a kidnapping, much less
all of this!

CHIEF NARMER
And what about the Foreigners continuing
to land in the Delta, are you also too
preoccupied to keep up with them?

KING SALO
(shouts)
I know everything that goes on in my
Empire. You think ships docking under the
shadow of night elude me. Caravans of
traders coming in from the east, and
leaving with fewer men is no secret. But I
am just an old man, getting by on
borrowed time. I must step back to see
who will step forth as a true ruler, with the
best interest for our Empire.

CHIEF NARMER
But my king you have plenty of time left,
surely you cannot just spend it as an
experiment to see who will evolve as the
Empire's next true ruler.

KING SALO
How about you? Have you changed your
mind, and decided to take your place as our
Empire's rightful ruler.

CHIEF NARMER
No I have not my king. A life in Nekheb
village, with my family and kinsmen is still
the only life for me.

KING SALO
Then until I see another who is at least half
the leader you are. An experiment, will my
last days be.

CHIEF NARMER
My King I have already explained to you
that, me accepting the crown will only
turn into a pattern of dreadful evil
turmoil, with plots on my life, and the
exploitation of the less fortunate to get
the crown back into the royal family. The
Empire does not need that right now.

KING SALO
No, what the Empire does not need is
another line of weak leaders, sitting on
the throne. If it wasn't for your great

grandfather Sakmra, this Empire would
not be as fortunate as we are today.

CHIEF NARMER
I am aware of the history of my great
grandfather Sakmra. I know what he has
done for this Empire. And just like him, I
do not want to sit on the throne.

KING SALO
(beat)
Those were different times then.
(beat)
Did you know my grandfather and father
fought in the war alongside Sakmra. My
grandfather was in the same unit as
Sakmra. After the war he spoke volumes of
Sakmra leading us to victory. Strategy after
strategy that Sakmra used to outwit the
invaders, how Sakmra sparked and
renewed the energy of all our warriors
throughout the war, the Empire loved him.

CHIEF NARMER
Yes, the Empire loved him during the war,
and then afterwards turned on him, with
his life being threatened by members of
the royal family. Where was his beloved
Empire then?

KING SALO
My grandfather, King Amu knew Sakmra
should have been crowned king after the
Empire's great victory. Amu spoke of it
numerous times. He spoke of it until his
dying day.
(beat)
As a boy I heard so much of Sakmra's
achievements, it was as if I walked with
him personally. Grandfather Amu knew
that Sakmra was the leader capable of
leading the Empire into the future.
(beat)
Sakmra was the one whom more than
anyone else, had proven that he deserved
to be King.

CHIEF NARMER

If so was the case, why did no one in the Empire speak up for Sakmra. Why didn't King Amu speak on his behalf?

KING SALO

Grandfather Amu knew what was going on, he was aware of the measures his uncles were taking to make sure the crown stayed in the family. Speaking on the matter would have been betraying the family, and certain death. Amu's life was in as much danger as anyone else who threatened the lineage.

CHIEF NARMER

(gets emotional)

Would you believe that Sakmra never wanted the crown. Sakmra was never upset that the royal family wanted the crown to stay at home. For him it was that an Empire that he did so much for would turn on him at the snap of a finger, as if there was no yesterday.

KING SALO

Yes, members of the royal family probably turned on Sakmra, but the Empire never turned on him. He never gave them the opportunity to choose. He stepped back without even an attempt at his throne.

(beat)

I remember the final years of my grandfather Amu after he left the throne. If there was anything that led him to an early grave, it was him wondering how could a born leader just turn and walk away from leading.

CHIEF NARMER

You will be surprised how easy it is to do, when you feel that those who you love and will be leading, have turned and walked away from you.

Beat.

KING SALO

Ok I will accept that being the reason for
Sakmra not accepting. Now what is your
reason?

CHIEF NARMER

Perhaps it is because my great
grandfather's blood runs through me. And
men, who turn and walk away, are all we
desire to be.

KING SALO

You are correct young ruler. Your
ancestor's blood does pump vigorously
through your heart. But you still have not
realized the traits and blessings they
passed on to you.

CHIEF NARMER

You must forgive me my King, but I did not
come bearing reasons or excuses. Only to
notify you of a meeting of the council to be
held at Nekheb hall, so that we could
address this ongoing feud between our
brothers the Aswans and the Mumons, also
to address the Foreigners steadfast
invasion. We must put an end to both issues
once and for all.

KING SALO

What other chief or elder of the council do
you think came here wanting to address the
landings, or the feud between our brothers.

CHIEF NARMER

They probably do not view the Foreigners
as a threat. And as for the feud, even you
yourself admitted that everything was good
just days ago.

KING SALO

And that.

> (beat)

That is what separates you young ruler. You recognize a problem and take the initiative to make a change. My nephews and sons have no intentions on benefiting the Empire outside of their own monetary gains. They cannot recognize that the Foreigners are strengthening to overthrow their Empire. All they see are new merchandise and expanding trade routes.

> (beat)

But you, you are like your great grandfather Sakmra. You could see the intentions of man, the Ntchru shines through you as they do one of the temple keepers, and you command the battlefield as the greatest of generals do. Young ruler you are a King. It is all in you. You are our Empire's true ruler. It is as if the Universe has preordained it for you.

CHIEF NARMER

> (declines)

My King your words are very flattering, and your offer as usual very tempting, but with all due respect my King you must understand that I cannot accept your offer, if there is a possibility that me being your successor might disrupt the peace in Tameri. In our beloved land!

KING SALO

That is why it must be you young ruler who is my successor. The members of the royal family who are in line do not care about the Empire. They are just fighting to sit on the throne. Before my grandfather Amu died he made me promise him that if I ever got the chance. That I was to make sure I put a true Ruler on the throne. Someone who will strengthen our Empire!

> (beat)

How about you help me keep a promise to
an admired ancestor, so that I could
transition a happy man, knowing that the
future of our nation is in the hands of a
leader who is capable of leading.

                    CHIEF NARMER
I am sorry my King but I must decline,
please bear with me. King Salo it has been
a pleasure seeing you again but I must
return to Nekheb, to meet with General
Fusa for a report of the damages from the
battle between the Aswans and the
Mumons.

King Salo holds a beat.

                    CHIEF NARMER
I trust you will be at the meeting nineteen
days from today, if your health permits.

King Salo stands.

                    KING SALO
I will be there. Chief Narmer it was good
seeing you again.

                    CHIEF NARMER
It was my honor and pleasure, my King.

                    KING SALO
I hope to get a visit from you again, before
it being another matter of duty.

                    CHIEF NARMER
I will see to it my King.

                    KING SALO
Have a safe journey home, and give my best
to your chief wife Berenib.

                    CHIEF NARMER
I will. And see to it that you get some
enjoyment in your few remaining years.

KING SALO
My best years are behind me young ruler.
My only obligation now is to name a fit
ruler, and you are my first and only option,
so I beg of you to at least consider my
proposition. Please just think it over.

CHIEF NARMER
I will. I promise you my King, I will.

KING SALO
Thank you. That is all I ask.

They nod to each other. Chief Narmer kneels goodbye. He stands and leaves the
study. He walks down a hallway. As Chief Narmer walks, PRINCE CHALA comes up
another hallway, and they cross paths. They stop to address each other.

PRINCE CHALA
Chief Narmer, it has been a while. How are
you doing?

CHIEF NARMER
Prince Chala, yes it has. I am good and
yourself?

They shake hands.

PRINCE CHALA
I am good. So what brings you to Thebes?
Have you finally decided to accept the old
man's offer?

CHIEF NARMER
No, I am leaving the weight of the Empire
on your shoulders. I think that you are
better built for it.

PRINCE CHALA
Nonsense, why do you think King Salo has
not offered the crown to any of the
members of the royal family as yet?
Rumors throughout the Empire have it
that you are his one and only choice to be
his successor.

                    CHIEF NARMER
That is just a ridiculous rumor. I have no
interest in being King, so how could I be
the only choice?

                    PRINCE CHALA
That is truly a shame. You would make an
exceptional King.

                    CHIEF NARMER
I thank you for your considerable praises
Prince Chala, but as I have said, I have no
interest in being King. I came here today
to request a meeting of the Council to be
held at the Nekheb Hall, to put an end to
the feud between our brothers the
Mumons and the Aswans.

                    PRINCE CHALA
I strongly support such a meeting, and
will be there to do my part, and assist you
in any way that I can to resolve this feud.

                    CHIEF NARMER
I truly would appreciate that, because this
matter has gotten way out of control. The
meeting will be held nineteen days from
today at the Nekheb hall.

Prince Chala nods.

                    PRINCE CHALA
I will be there.

They shake hands again.

                    CHIEF NARMER
I look forward to seeing you there. Until
then, take care.

They nod to each other once again and part ways. Chief Narmer walks down the
steps, and heads back to Nekheb.

EXT. KING'S PALACE IN THEBES - DAY

Chief Narmer comes down the stairs, mounts his horse and rides away.

EXT. MUMON'S VILLAGE - DAY

Fusa and COMPANY all on horses ride to the battle scene of the Aswans and the Mumons War. When they arrive at the edge of the village, they immediately notice the devastation. Injured fighters, dead bodies, and burning buildings. VILLAGERS weep and mourn everywhere.

The ASWAN WARRIORS notice Fusa as he approaches and stand to greet him. Fusa notices that the Mumons are being held captive.

The MUMON CHIEF JUSA is held to the side, isolated from the rest of his warriors. He is being treated better than the rest of his Villagers.

Fusa rides through all the commotion, and goes over and addresses the Aswan Chief Duba.

                    FUSA
               (jokes)
          Well, it is obvious I do not have to ask you,
          how are things going?

                    DUBA
          You could, but sometimes life explains
          itself.

They bow in mutual respect.

                    DUBA
          General Fusa, it is an honor as usual despite
          this current situation.

                    FUSA
          Thank you Chief Duba, it is always good
          seeing you. But I must admit, it is this
          current situation that brings me here today.

                    DUBA
          How convenient. Now there is a reaction
          from the council. Where was the council
          when the Mumons continuously crossed the
          given borders into our land, harassing and
          forcing the Aswan residence off of our land?
          Where was the council a week ago, when the
          Mumons kidnapped the three young women
          as they were fetching water from the river?

FUSA

No, I did not come with a message from the council, but instead with a message to the council, of which you are a seated member. Chief Narmer is requesting a meeting with all the members of the council, to finally put an end to this ongoing feud between yourselves and the Mumons.

DUBA

That is fine with me. Justice must be served to the families of the three victims.

FUSA

Are you sure it was the Mumons who committed the act?

DUBA

They were seen dragging the young women away, plus we recovered one of the women being held here to be sold.

FUSA

Did you? What kind of condition was she in?

DUBA

She had been raped and beaten, but still alive. Even so...

He points to the Mumons.

DUBA

She is in a much better position, than the one these unworthy barbarians have found themselves in because I assure you, if the Mumons do not reimburse my people sufficiently for our losses, including my soldiers. They will all negotiate the pointed tip of my spare, or be sold as slaves.

FUSA

Please do not haste to any action, let us wait to see what decision the council and the throne comes up with.

                    DUBA
Like I said that is fine by me, but until then
they stay in my possession.

                    FUSA
That is between you and the Mumons, but I
trust you will have Chief Jusa at the meeting.

                    DUBA
He will be there.

                    FUSA
Good. Chief Narmer has requested a
meeting at the Nekheb hall, nineteen days
from today.

                    DUBA
I will be there.

                    FUSA
Thank you.

Fusa bows.

                    FUSA
As usual, Chief Duba, it was good seeing
you again, but I must be on my way now.
Please be careful and stay out of harm's
way.

                    DUBA
Stay strong my friend.

Fusa mounts his horse.

                    DUBA
I will friend, and you do the same.

Fusa turns to ride away when Duba asks.

                    DUBA
Will you be addressing Chief Jusa on your
way out?

                    FUSA
It would only be right.

They nod to each other before Fusa leaves. Duba signals to his GUARD to let Fusa speak to Chief Jusa.

Fusa rides up, gets off his horse, and walks over to Jusa then bows in respect.

                            JUSA
I hope you are here to put an end to this injustice by the Aswans, who have raided my village, and are now holding us all captive.

                            FUSA
I will take no part in this matter until the council has made their decision.

                            JUSA
No one should need the council to see that this is unacceptable. One tribe has not held another captive in over two hundred years.

                            FUSA
The Aswans felt they had enough reasons to go to war, and now you are a prisoner of that war. I have no authority over someone's prisoner.

                            JUSA
But clearly nothing could justify them taking an entire village as their prisoners.

                            FUSA
I do agree, but this conflict the council will have to resolve, not me. Chief Narmer is requesting a council meeting to put an end to this foolishness once and for all. The meeting will be held at the Nekheb hall, nineteen days from today.

                            JUSA
In nineteen days, and what am I to do until then?

                    FUSA
You speak as if the Mumon people are
guilty of nothing. What about the three
women your men kidnapped?

                    JUSA
I knew nothing of it.

                    FUSA
One of the women was found here in your
village. How could you not have known?

Jusa tries to cover his guilt.

                    JUSA
I hear rumors of the three women being
taken from the river, and the Mumon's men
were suspected. I investigated the rumors.
          (beat)
But every man assured me that they knew
or heard nothing of it.

                    FUSA
How could you, the Chief of the village, not
find out that three kidnapped women are
being raped and sold under your watch?

                    JUSA
I trusted the word of my men, and
continues on with my affairs as Chief.

                    FUSA
Now let's see, do your brothers of the
council trust your words? Until then, I
suggest you think of what you are willing to
part with to stay alive.

Fusa bows in respect.

                    JUSA
Well it seems as if I have no other options.

                    FUSA
I will see you in nineteen days.

Fusa mounts his horse and leaves.

JUSA
(to General Masa)
You let the lad know he is to take full
responsibility for the three women.

GENERAL MASA nods. A YOUNG WARRIOR takes notice of Chief Jusa and General Masa as they talk to each other.

Fusa looks around at the damage to the Mumon village as he rides out.

Duba stands, and watch Fusa and company as they ride off into the distance.

EXT. OUTSIDE SAIS - DAY

Ben, Jaugen, Srtife, and Alsi pass some impressive sites on their way Sais. Several different little communities sprung up along the coast with an equal mix of races.

Alsi and Srtife observe people in their daily activities. They see the statues and monuments alongside streets paved with stones.

EXT. SAIS - DAY

They arrive at Sais. Ben stops and they dismount their horses. They walk through an entrance, which leads them to a courtyard with a few large houses.

EXT. COURTYARD - DAY

Ben walks over to one of the houses and addresses the MAN standing guard.

BEN
(nods)
I am here to see Beirut.

BEIRUT'S GUARD
Wait here a moment.

The guard goes inside.

ALSI
What is this place?

                          BEN
          This is Sais and these are the Saite leaders.
          Some of the richest Foreigners in the Nile
          Valley, they are the ones to see when we
          need to get something done.

                          JAUGEN
          I will be outside by the horses.

Jaugen exits the courtyard.

INT. BEIRUT HOUSE - DAY

BEIRUT is inside, getting pampered by a room full of women, when his Guard walks
in.

                     BEIRUT'S GUARD
          Pardon me sir. Ben is here to see you.

                         BEIRUT
          That's marvelous. Bring him in.

The guard leaves.

EXT. BEIRUT HOUSE - CONTINUOUS

                          BEN
          See that man over there?

Ben points to a MAN across the way.

                          BEN
          That's KALILI his ancestors have been here
          for over seven generations. They helped to
          build this community. From once only a
          trading post, to now a place of residence.
          At one time us Foreigners were only
          permitted to sell or buy here in this
          country. But trade ventures often lead to
          Foreigners staying overnight, or for days
          at a time. Which led to the occasional tents
          popping up, which eventually evolved into
          secured stone structure, and over
          generations we now have this community.

                         ALSI
            Is this the only community like this?

                         BEN
            No, there are several communities like this
            along the Mediterranean Sea coast.

Beirut's Guard walks out.

                    BEIRUT'S GUARD
                       (to Ben)
            Come with me.

INT. BEIRUT HOUSE - CONTINUOUS

They follow the Guard inside. He leads them to Beirut.

                        BEIRUT
            Ben, it is good to see you again. Even
            better to see that you are a man of your
            word.

Ben shakes Beirut's hand.

                         BEN
            I assured you that I would be here.

                        BEIRUT
            Yes, you did. But when one sees you with
            fast Jaugen, a man doesn't know what to
            make of your character. I know you own
            him, but if people see you with him, they
            will start to identify you with him. A low
            life good for nothing!

                         BEN
            I like to think that, I am my own man.

Ben pays Beirut.

                        BEIRUT
            You seem intelligent enough to know that,
            often in life it is not what you think of
            yourself, but what people think of you,
            that get you ahead in life.
                       (to his Guard)

Weigh this.

BEN
Let me worry about my reputation as of
now.

BEIRUT
(nods)
Are these the two that came across?

BEN
(nods)
Yes, they are. This is my cousin Alsi, and his
son Srtife.

They shake Beirut's hand.

BEIRUT
Welcome to opportunity gentlemen.

ALSI
Thank you.

SRTIFE
We greatly appreciate it.

BEIRUT
Would you gentlemen like some
refreshments?

SRTIFE
Yes, thank you.

BEIRUT
(to a Servant)
Get these gentlemen some refreshments.

Beirut's SERVANT finishes weighing the gold and nods.

BEIRUT
The ever-sharp Ben from exporting seeds
and grains, to now importing fellow
countrymen. You keep this up you could
evolve into a very important man in this
country. Come and have a drink with me.

                              BEN
              I would love to, but I must decline. I am
              trying to make it back to Buba before
              nightfall, you understand.

                              BEIRUT
              Certainly.

They shake hands.

                              BEN
              I cannot thank you enough. Your services
              are sincerely appreciated.

                              BEIRUT
              Don't mention it. Have a safe journey
              home, and don't be a stranger. If you ever
              have any problems, whatever it may be,
              just come and see me.

                              BEN
              I will. It is good to know that you are here
              if I may ever need you. Once again, thank
              you.

Ben walks away while Srtife and Alsi say their respectful farewells. They leave
behind Ben.

EXT. NEKHEB VILLAGE - DAY

Fusa and company rides back into Nekheb. The LOCALS looks on at them. They
make the horses trot through the town, rather than gallop.

The village is prosperous. As they pass you see beautiful houses, trading post,
buildings, arts and crafts, streets paved with bricks and monuments.

Fusa rides up to Narmer palace and hands his horse to a handler. He walks upstairs.

INT. NARMER'S PALACE - DAY

Chief Narmer waits for Fusa in the study. Fusa comes in and bows.

                              FUSA
              Hail the Chief.

CHIEF NARMER
(nodding)
Welcome, what is the status of the Aswans
and the Mumons?

FUSA
It is not looking good. Almost half of the
Mumons men are dead. The other half, are
being held as prisoners. The Aswans took
substantial losses and injuries, but nothing
close to that of the Mumons. And now
Chief Duba is demanding to be
compensated for their loss, or they will kill
every Mumons in their possession, or sell
them as slaves. But Chief Duba has agreed
not to take any action, until the ruling from
the council.

CHIEF NARMER
Did you notify the other members of the
council about the meeting?

FUSA
I have messengers in route to every
member of the council as we speak. We
should be hearing replies anytime now.
What was the reaction from the Throne?

CHIEF NARMER
King Salo and Prince Chala said they would
be here to help us come to a resolution.
But as usual, King Salo was only concerned
with naming me his successor.

FUSA
Did you say yes this time?

The way Chief Narmer looks at Fusa, indicates "no."

FUSA
Why on earth not? There is no one in this
entire Empire more fit to rule. What is
stopping you?

CHIEF NARMER

I have told you before. I have no intention on interfering with the affairs of the royal family.

FUSA

This is not the affairs of the royal family, but that of the Kushite Empire. There is not one member of the royal family that does not have ulterior motives for the Throne.

CHIEF NARMER

If even so be the case. Now is not the time to start a possible conflict in the Empire. That will only weaken and divide the Empire.

FUSA

There would be no division. There is not a single man in the entire Empire that is more qualified to be King.

CHIEF NARMER

It is not the common man that I am referring to, but the over looked members of the royal family. The overlooked members, who will go to any measures to exploit the common man to serve their desire.

A Guard walks in with a message from the council.

N GUARD 1

Pardon me chief. There is a messenger outside with a message from the council.

CHIEF NARMER

Send him in.

A MESSENGER walks in and, kneels.

MESSENGER

Greetings Chief. Greetings General. I am back with a reply from Chief Mnfeco, of Hierak.

                    CHIEF NARMER
          Good. What is the reply from Chief Mnfeco?

                    MESSENGER
          Chief Mnfeco said to inform you that he
          would be here. He also said, he is very
          pleased that someone is taking the
          initiative to solve this problem, and he will
          do all he can to assist.

                    CHIEF NARMER
          Thank you. That will be all.

                    MESSENGER
          Thank you my Chief. And thank you also my
          general.
                    (he leaves)

                    FUSA
                    (to Narmer)
          I seriously think if you have the best
          interest of the Empire in mind, you should
          accept the offer from the King. It is only
          right.

                    CHIEF NARMER
                    (dismissive)
          Let us handle one problem at a time. Right
          now the Aswans and the Mumons conflict,
          is the issue at hand.

Fusa, disappointed, nods in agreement.

EXT. VILLAGES - DAY

MONTAGE:

-Different MESSENGERS, carrying the Nekheb flag, goes to various MEMBERS OF
THE COUNCIL.

-They address the CHIEFS, ELDERS, and TEMPLE KEEPERS of every village. They all
nod in agreement.

-They mount their horses and deliver the replies back to Chief Narmer at Nekheb
village.

EXT. BUBA VILLAGE - DAY

Alsi and Srtife gazes at all the amazing sites along the way. They are amazed as they pass through the different villages. They see a mixture of all cultures and PEOPLE OF ALL RACES with CHILDREN. They pass straight through to Ben's house.

Ben's wife, BLOSSOM, stands outside to greet them. Jaugen separates from the group and goes to the outhouse where he lives. They get off their horses.

                    BLOSSOM
               (hugs and kiss Ben)
          Welcome home my love. I have been
          missing you.

                    BEN
          Thank you my love, I have missed you also.
          This is my cousin Alsi and his firstborn son
          Srtife.
               (to Alsi and Srtife)
          And as you both could see, this is my
          beautiful wife Blossom.

Blossom shakes their hands.

                    BLOSSOM
          Welcome. It is good to meet you both, I
          have heard so much of you Alsi, it is a
          pleasure to finally meet you.

                    ALSI
          The pleasure is mine. With such beauty it
          is easy to see how you have captured the
          heart of my cousin.

                    BLOSSOM
          I see your reputation accurately depicts
          you.

                    ALSI
          I only hope it did me justice. Often when
          one's reputation precedes them, the
          individual is received under false
          assumptions.

                          BLOSSOM
            I assure you, justice was served.

                            BEN
            Come let us go inside, and get you two
            settled in.

They walk toward the door as Ben and Blossom show their affection for one
another.

INT. BEN'S HOUSE - DAY

DADE, Ben's youngest son runs toward him.

                           DADE
            Father, father.

                            BEN
                     (picks him up)
            How is my little man doing?

                           DADE
            Where have you been? I have not seen you
            in two days.

                            BEN
            I went to meet my cousin.

                           DADE
                      (excitedly)
            You have a cousin. I had no idea. Why have
            I never met him?

                            BEN
            Well, let me introduce you. This is your
            uncle Alsi and his son, your cousin, Srtife.
                     (to Alsi and Srtife)
            And this is my bodyguard, my youngest
            son Dade.

                           ALSI
            Greetings little Dade, it is an honor to meet
            you.

                    DADE
Since you two are family, do I have to
protect you two also?

                    SRTIFE
        (shakes Dade's hand)
Only if you are not too busy protecting the
rest of the family.

                    DADE
I will see what I can do.

                    BEN
        (tickles Dade)
You will see what you could do, you little
tyrant you.

Dade laughs.

                    BEN
What will I ever do with you? Where are
your brother and sisters?

                    DADE
They are out back doing their chores.

                    BEN
Go and fetch them. Tell them to come and
meet their uncle and cousin.

                    DADE
Okay.

Ben puts Dade down, he runs off shouting.

                    DADE
Marcus! Myia! Lena!

                    ALSI
He resembles Kevin as a child.

                    BEN
Sometimes I myself see the similarity.
Come, leave your loads here. Let me
introduce you to my other wife.

Srtife and Alsi put their loads down and follow Ben into the kitchen where ANN is cooking over a wooden fire. She sees them coming and stands up to greet them.

                         ANN
              How are you doing, my love?

                         BEN
              I am good, thank you. This is my cousin
              Alsi and his son Srtife.

                         ANN
              Greetings gentlemen. I welcome you both
              Alsi and Srtife.

She shakes their hands.

                         ANN
              We have been expecting you.

                         ALSI
              Another beautiful wife, cousin you are a
              fortunate man.

Ann blushes. The CHILDREN walks in.

                         BEN
              Ah, yes. And these are the rest of my
              children.

He points to introduce each of his children as they walk over.

                         BEN
              This is Lena, my oldest. Marcus, and Myia.

LENA and Srtife makes eye contact.

                         BEN
              Children, this is my cousin Alsi and his son
              Srtife.

MARCUS shakes their hands.

                         MARCUS
              Welcome to our home.

Lena keeps eye contact with Srtife, and gives him a seductive look as she introduces herself.

                    LENA
                (seductively)
            Welcome.

MYIA greets them next, shakes their hands.

                    MYIA
            Welcome to our home.

                    BLOSSOM
            Okay children. Go get yourselves ready for
            supper.

As they're leaving, Ben stops Marcus.

                    BEN
            Marcus. Go and invite Jaugen and Rose to
            come join us for dinner.

                    MARCUS
            Okay father.

                    ANN
            I hope you gentlemen have an appetite,
            because we have prepared a feast for your
            arrival.

                    SRTIFE
            I'm starved. I could eat an entire cow by
            myself.

                    ANN
            That's good. Dinner will be served shortly.

                    BEN
            Okay fellows, come let me get you two
            comfortable for your first home-cooked
            meal in your new home.

They all walk to the table.

                         ALSI
         Cousin I must say I envy you, two beautiful
         wives and four wonderful children. My
         respect goes out to you.

INT. BEN'S HOUSE - LATER

                         JAUGEN
         I mean exactly as he was about to snatch
         the sheep, there stood our family dog Rex,
         staring him directly in the eyes.

Everyone laughs.

                         JAUGEN
                    (laughing)
         As he turned to run, Rex grabbed onto his
         behind ripping away both flesh and
         clothing.

They laugh again.

                         JAUGEN
         He hopped away holding his behind,
         screaming for dear life.

Continues laughing.

                         ALSI
         I barely got away from that bloody dog. I
         couldn't sit down for a couple seasons.

                         JAUGEN
                    (still laughing)
         My father loved that story, he told it for
         years.

Everyone except Srtife and Lena laughs along. They just admire each other.

                         BEN
         I remember those times. It seems as if it
         was only yesterday.

                         ANN
         It sounds as if while growing up in your
         old country, Alsi you were quite a handful.

ALSI

I have not as yet gotten my opportunity to
be a handful, because of Jaugen's family
dog Rex I haven't attempted to steal a
sheep since the age of ten.

BEN
(laughing)
Yea, that is true. Afterwards he only stole
cows, pigs, chickens, and so forth.

ALSI

I must confess I was quite the scoundrel.
Anything that was eatable and not tied to a
peg, it was as if I felt I had part ownership.
It got to the point, that when anything in
the community was missing, I was one of
the first suspects.

ANN

How did you ever stay alive with such a
reputation?

ALSI

I out grew it at an early age. By age
seventeen, that life was completely behind
me.

Blossom notices that Srtife and Lena cannot stop looking at each other.

BLOSSOM
(to Lena)
Would you two like a personal portrait of
each other?

LENA
(shyly)
No Ma 'am.

SRTIFE

You must pardon me Ma 'am. I am just not
use to seeing someone with such beauty.

                    BLOSSOM
There is nothing wrong with admiration,
but you two look at each other as if you
desire to take each other right here and
now.

                    LENA
              (embarrassed)
Mother.

                    SRTIFE
Not at all ma'am, I beg of you to please
pardon me Ma 'am if I have offended you.

                    BEN
Darling, let the children be. Please.

                    BLOSSOM
I am just saying, there are ways of making
a respectable gesture.

Lena disregards her mother.

                    LENA
So. Srtife how was your trip here.

                    SRTIFE
It was very rough. It took roughly two
weeks to get here, even though I lost count
of the days on about the 4th or 5th. That
was the longest I have ever been on a boat.
We survived on only water and bread.
Over three hundred people packed onto a
boat only fit for a hundred. If it were not
for the dream of landing in Kush, a lot
more of the men would have died along
the way.

                    LENA
What do you mean a lot more? Were there
casualties along the way?

                    SRTIFE
A few here and there. There was this one
man who died of dehydration. His lips
turned purple....

                            JAUGEN
                Okay, okay son that is enough. We're
                eating here, are you trying to make us lose
                our appetite. Come, let us have a toast to
                your dreams coming true, to you both
                sitting here safely in your new home, in
                Kush.

Srtife and Lena still admires each other as everyone lifts their mugs to a toast.
Everyone takes a sip and toast again to the future. It's a good time.

EXT. BUBA VILLAGE - DAY

-MONTAGE

Srtife and Lena get to know each other better. They go for a walk after dinner. Srtife
picks a flower and hands it to Lena. She smells it and takes his hand. They walk off
together.

Along their walk Srtife climbs a fruit tree and picks fruit for Lena. They sit and eat
them together. Lena playfully smashes one on Srtife's face, then points at him and
laughs. He tries to get her back.

Srtife chases Lena in a meadow. Srtife tackles Lena, they roll around in flowers
playing and enjoying each other's company. He gets on top of her to kiss her, but
instead of a kiss he gets another piece of fruit smashed in my face.

She laughs, gets up, and runs away. They laugh and run and play together in bliss.

INT. BEN'S HOUSE - DAY

Jaugen, Ben and Alsi sit and reminisce. Everyone is once again at the dinner table,
laughing and eating.

EXT. RIVER - DAY

Srtife and Lena goes horseback riding. They ride to a beautiful river and decide to go
swimming. They get closer physically, but nothing sexual happens.

INT. BEN'S HOUSE - DAY

The entire family is eating dinner again. Everyone is laughing and enjoying them-
selves.

EXT. MEADOW - DAY

Lena and Srtife sit in a meadow and sip wine next to their horses, as they watch the sunset.

Lena takes Srtife's face and turns it toward her. They look into each other's eyes and kiss. The sun sets behind them.

INT. NARMER'S BEDROOM – DAY

THE DAY OF THE MEETING OF THE COUNCIL. Chief Narmer's eyes opens to the sound of a ROOSTER'S crow. He sits up on the edge of the bed. Berenib reaches over and rubs his back.

                    CHIEF NARMER
          Good morning.

                    BERENIB
          Good morning.

He gets up and walks to the balcony to look over his village. Berenib hugs him from behind.

                    BERENIB
          Are you okay, my love?

                    CHIEF NARMER
          Yes, I am fine. I just hope to put an end to
          all of this today.

                    BERENIB
          I am sure you will. The rest of the Empire
          is just as tired of this as you are.

                    CHIEF NARMER
          I only hope so. Could you go and see to it
          that Djer is up and ready to go?

                    BERENIB
          Certainly my love.

She turns Chief Narmer around.

                    BERENIB
          Do not worry about anything. I am sure
          everything will go just fine.

Berenib kisses him on the cheek then puts on her robe as she leaves the room.

INT. DJER'S DOOR/ROOM - DAY

Berenib knocks on Djer's door.

> DJER
> (brushes his teeth)
> Come in.

He looks at her.

> BERENIB
> Good morning my son, your father told me
> to come and make sure that you are up and
> ready to go.

He gargles and spits.

> DJER
> Good morning mother, I am finishing up
> now.

He kisses her.

> DJER
> How are you, mother?

> BERENIB
> I am fine.

She looks around.

> BERENIB
> It has been so long since I have been in
> your room. You have everything arranged
> so differently.

> DJER
> Yes. My interest has changed, as I have
> gotten older.

> BERENIB
> Really, and what are your interest these
> days.

DJER

Gorgeous women and painting portraits of
them.

Djer smiles as he hands his mother some samples of his work.

BERENIB
(looks at the paintings)
I see, very interesting.

She puts them on the bed.

BERENIB

Your father has been taking you to council
meetings since the age of seven, surely you
have other interest than just painting
portraits.

DJER

No need to worry mother, my people are
still my first love and priority. I only paint
portraits to pass time.

BERENIB

Your father expects a lot from you. So let
us not make mention of your hobbies, only
of what he wants to hear.

DJER

I know mother.

BERENIB

That's good.

She fixes his clothes.

BERENIB

Your father will be along shortly.

She kisses him proudly.

BERENIB

Your father and I are very proud of you
son.

She leaves the room. Djer sits, and waits for his father. Narmer comes along and greets him.

                         DJER
            Good morning father.

Narmer hands Djer a scroll.

                    CHIEF NARMER
            Good morning my son.

They walk off together.

INT. NEKHEB GREETING HALL - DAY

All THE MEMBERS OF THE COUNCIL are in the Nekheb greeting hall socializing with each other. Duba and Jusa are in separate corners, pleading their cases to whom-ever will listen.

All the temple keepers are socializing together. Chief Narmer and Djer enters the room and goes around and greets everyone.

King Salo and Prince Chala enter the room. The King gets a round of applause. All the Chief's and Elders individually comes over and kneel to greet the King.

                       SERVANT
            Breakfast is ready to be served.

The entire council walks into the dining hall.

INT. DINING HALL - CONTINUOUS

Everyone sits and enjoy breakfast. After breakfast they all get up and go into the conference hall.

INT. CONFERENCE HALL - CONTINUOUS

A DRUM sounds to address the room.

                       SPEAKER
            Greetings my brothers, greetings to you all.
            We the council of elders, chiefs, temple
            keepers, and throne of the Kushite Empire,
            were asked to come here today by Chief
            Narmer. We were called here to do our
            duty as a nation, and as a nation we will

once and for all put an end to this ongoing
feud between our brothers the Aswans
and the Mumons.

Everyone cheers. Chief Narmer takes the scroll from Djer and walks to the podium.

                    CHIEF NARMER
Greetings my brothers. All praises are due
to the Ntchru for gathering us all here today
safely and for giving us all another chance
at life. Because of their principles and laws
all thing are possible. I have asked you all
here today, with intentions on us putting an
end to this war between our brothers. But
even more important, for us to come to an
agreement that from this day forth, there
will be no more wars, between no two
villages of this Empire. In these times we
ourselves are our biggest obstacles. We
must abandon our self-destructing ways
and stand together, to strengthen our
Empire.

A round of applause.

                    CHIEF NARMER
If nothing else, let us all take this
declaration from our gathering here today,
thank you.

He steps down.

                    MNFECO
                (stands, and applaud)
I Chief Mnfeco of the Hierak Village,
support this proposal.

                    BOBO
                (stands, and applaud)
I Chief Bobo of Meroe, also support this
proposal.

                    MUMBA
                (applauds)
As do it.

The SPEAKER beats the drum to gain control of the room, and stop all of the, outbursts as he walk back to the podium.

                    RASA
          I Chief Rasa of Napata and the Napata
          Village, also support this declaration of
          peace by Chief Narmer.

Everyone erupts in cheers again. The Speaker beats the DRUM to calm them down.

                    SPEAKER
          Settle down. Settle down. Control your-
          selves. It is safe to say that we all support
          this declaration, of peace by Chief Narmer.

Everyone cheers. The Speaker beats the DRUM again.

                    SPEAKER
          Agreed. So it is. Now let us get back to the
          reason why we 're here today, to bring the
          order of Ma 'at to our brothers the
          Mumons and the Aswans. Thank you. At
          this time, I ask both Chief Jusa of the
          Mumon village and Chief Duba of the
          Aswan village to please take a stand.

Both Chiefs stand.

                    SPEAKER
          We the council of the Kushite Empire are
          gathered here today to hear the length of
          your conflict. Which will be follow by a
          deliberation, then a solution from the
          council, on how this matter will be
          resolved. A decision that you will both
          abide by, as members of the council of this
          empire. Do you both understand this
          procedure?

                    DUBA
          I do.

                    JUSA
          I do.

                    SPEAKER
With that understood, I now ask you both
Chief Duba and Chief Jusa to please take
your seats on the Podium.

Both Chiefs walk to the podium and take their seats.

                    SPEAKER
Thank you. You will both get your
opportunity to give your account of the
conflict. And from your statements, the
council will draw their conclusion to see
who will be compensated for their
people's afflictions. Do you both
understand this procedure?

                    JUSA
I do.

                    DUBA
I do.

                    SPEAKER
Okay then, let us begin with you, Chief Jusa.

                    JUSA
Thank you, this has been a serious case of
injustice. Or at the very least, a big
misunderstanding.

                    DUBA
          (burst out)
The only misunderstanding is me not
knowing why I spared your worthless life.

                    SPEAKER
          (beat his drum)
Restrain yourself. An outburst like that is
unacceptable. Humble yourself, and allow
the council to get to the bottom of this
situation. Go ahead Chief Jusa carry on.

                    JUSA
Thank you. As I was saying, this has just
been one big unfortunate
misunderstanding. Starting with the three

young women being kidnapped, which I knew nothing about.

                    SPEAKER
You must admit. There was much more that lead up to this than just the kidnappings. And how could such an act be committed by your kinsmen, and you know nothing of it.

                    JUSA
The other acts were of no major offense.

                    DUBA
He only considers them to be of no major offense, because it was Mumons committing the act. Constantly disregarding the original ruling made by the council.

                    SPEAKER
Okay let us hear from you Chief Duba. What do you consider to be the cause of this confusion?

                    DUBA
This confusion stems from the Mumons continuous disregard for our given borders. For years they have been trespassing onto the Aswan's land to do their hunting, even more so after the council reassured the given borders.

                    JUSA
The Mumon population is larger than that of the Aswans, so we need a little extra range to do our hunting.

                    DUBA
Your population being larger has nothing to do with the Aswan people, and our given birth right. You and the Mumons being a larger population also have almost twice the land size as the Aswans, but still you hunt on our land.

SPEAKER
(to Jusa)
A ruling was made by the council,
clarifying the legally respected borders.
Why wasn't the ruling respected by your
Mumon people?

JUSA
The Mumons sometimes in our hunt for
food, stray across the designated borders
in our pursuit. It was meant as no
disrespect to the Aswans or the Council.

DUBA
Their disregard is in no pursuit for food. It
is to meet the Saite's demands for fur.
Continually the Mumons are in the
Aswan's territory antagonizing our people.
And now their uncivilized disregard for
others, have left two families mourning
over three young women.

SPEAKER
(to Jusa)
Once again how could three women be
kidnapped, and held captive in your
village, and you know nothing of it.
Especially when there are rumors,
accusing your kinsmen of this alleged act.
How could you the Chief, not find out if the
rumors are true?

JUSA
I did a thorough investigation at the time,
but everyone said they knew nothing of it
and said it was just rumors. It turns out the
three young men who committed the act,
had an oath so tight, that no one else in the
entire village knew anything of it. So when
everyone told me that they knew nothing
of it, they seem so sincere, I believed them.
I had no reason not to. Nothing like this
has ever happened since I have been Chief.

                    SPEAKER
Three women are dragged in, held as
prisoners, and no one sees or hears
nothing.
                    (beat)
How did you ever find out who did it?

Jusa glances at General Masa.

                     JUSA
After the invasion, and one of the young
women were found. One of the kidnapers
came forward and admitted to it. He also
confessed that his two accomplices had
been killed during the battle against the
Aswans.

The Council doesn't seem to believe him.

                    MUMBA
          (whispers to Rasa)
I don't believe a word he is saying.

                 GENERAL RASA
How could anyone, he is obviously lying.

                     JUSA
             (sympathetically)
I would like to apologize to the families of
the three young women, and to the entire
Aswan village. I will also faithfully abide by
any decision the council make to
reimburse their families. But surely
something must be done about the Aswans
invading, killing, and holding my entire
village as hostage.

                     DUBA
I care not for your apologies. I am here,
only to see justice served for the two
families of the three women. And for
everyone who have been victimized by
your uncivilized barbarianism.

SPEAKER
(to Duba)
Ma'at justice will be served. But in accord
with the order of Ma 'at, you will free the
Mumon population. This Empire will not
allow you to hold an entire village as your
prisoners.

JUSA
I thank you Saba speaker, but once again I
must retort that despite Chief Duba's
personal feelings towards me. My kinsmen
are wrong of nothing, other than the three
kidnaped women.

DUBA
(laughs in disagreement)
Ha ha ha! You wish. I have lost over a
thousand men in our battle, including my
wife's brother. I promise you, if my people
are not compensated for our losses. I will
kill every Mumon in my possession.

A LOUD GASP comes from the council. They whisper amongst themselves. The
Speaker beats his drum.

SPEAKER
(to Duba)
Such language will not be tolerated. Please
keep your personal feelings to yourself.
And just so that we are clear, the Mumon
people will be released.

JUSA
The Mumons lost ten times the amount of
fighters as the Aswans, surely I cannot be
held accountable for you attacking us.

DUBA
If it were not for the kidnapping, there
would not have been an attack in the first
place.

SPEAKER
(beats his drum)
I order you both to calm down. This
council will not have the both of you
arguing back and forth at each other. Now
Chief Duba what compensation would you
consider to be Ma'at justice for you and
your people.

DUBA
That is a decision I will leave up to the
council to make. I just ask the council to
keep in mind everyone who has been
affected in my village, because of the
continuous disregard and violations of the
Mumons.

SPEAKER
Fair enough. And how about you Chief Jusa,
What would you consider to be Ma 'at
justice for you and the Mumon people?

JUSA
That is a decision I too will leave up to the
council. I just ask the council to see that
the Aswans are not the only victims here.
The innocent Mumon Citizens who are
currently being wrongfully held as
prisoners by the Aswan warriors are the
real victims.

SPEAKER
The Council will consider both arguments
in there entirety, and use them to make
their decision. Is there anything else either
of you would like to add in your defense.

DUBA
No, that is all.

JUSA
No, I have nothing further to add. I just ask
that the principles of Ma 'at justice guide
the council's decision.

SPEAKER

Okay then with no further statements, I ask you both Chief Duba and Chief Jusa to please wait outside, while the council deliberate and make their decision.

TWO GUARDS escort Chief Duba and Chief Jusa outside.

SPEAKER

We have heard the weight of their testimony, now let us consult amongst ourselves to make a balance decision, and put an end to this feud.

He beats the drum one last time. The council begins to talk amongst them-selves.

SRCO

I clearly think Jusa and the Mumons are at fault. They should have to reimburse the Aswan tribe.

PRINCE CHALA

How could it clearly be their fault, when it takes two parties to be a war!

SRCO

True it takes two to war, but if it were not for the Mumons constant provoking, there would have never been a conflict in the first place.

PRINCE CHALA

Yes, the Mumons did provoke the conflict, but the Aswans in retaliation attack the Mumon's entire village, and who was not killed were all captured, and held as prisoners. I am not saying the Mumons did not provoke it, but the Aswans were no helpless victims.

ZOMI

I also feel the conflict was instigated by the Mumons antics, but raiding another's village, and holding them all as prisoners is a serious offense. And should not be overlooked!

KING SALO
Yes, It is an unacceptable offense, but what else was Chief Duba to do in his position.

ZOMI
Wait on an investigation from the council.

MUMBA
Wait on the council! I feel ashamed to say so, but the Council's reaction is slower than that of a snail. Waiting on the council was most likely what the Mumons were hoping for, to give them enough time to sell all the women.

MNFECO
I for one do not think the Aswans were wrong for attacking them. The Mumons are fortunate they are only being held as prisoners, because I would have killed them all.

SPEAKER
Please let us stay calm, and make a rational decision please.

POPA
There is no way I think it was appropriate for the Aswans to wage war on an entire village, over the kidnapping of three women.

BOBO
And what do you suppose Chief Duba should have done to seek justice for his people?
          (He gets no answer.)

CHIEF NARMER
Seeing the outcome of the Aswans attack, I don't think no one could say it was absolutely the right thing to do. But Duba being the Chief of the Aswan people, he was appointed to guarantee the safety of and justice for his people. And if one of us

could sit here and fault Chief Duba for fighting for his people, then that person should look within them-selves and ask yourself, for whom or why do you serve.

There is a silence in the room.

                    CHIEF NARMER
          I don't think the question should be who is
          wrong, because they both have committed
          acts which are widely unacceptable. But
          what is the measure of each offense, what
          precipitated it, and who are the real
          victim?

                    RASA
          I agree, they both were wrong, but they
          both cannot be compensated, so let us
          agree on who is the real victim, and what
          is reasonable compensation for the victim.

Everyone nods.

                    SPEAKER
          Okay then, a show of hands from all who
          thinks the Mumons are the blame for this
          conflict.

Ten village representatives raise their hands while the Speaker counts them.

                    SPEAKER
          Okay, and now a show of hands from all
          who thinks the Aswans had no right to
          rage a war.

Three village representatives raise their hands while the Speaker counts them.

                    SPEAKER
          All right then, the majority have spoken.
          Ruling goes in favor of the Aswan tribe.
          And with that conclusion let us now agree
          on what will be sufficient compensation
          for the Aswan village, and the families of
          the three young women.

POPA
And what will be the justice for the Mumon
village who are all currently being held as
prisoners.

MNFECO
From my perspective allowing them to
keep their lives is sufficient justice.

SPEAKER
(beats his drum)
I have asked you all to please disregard
your personal feelings. Any more
inappropriate outburst I will have to ask
the individual to leave. Now if you two are
through, could we finish making a ruling
on this matter? Thank you.

INT. WAITING ROOM AREA - CONTINUOUS

Duba and Jusa sit at separate ends of the hallway with separate GUARDS attending
to them.

Duba enjoys the view from a window overlooking the city, while Jusa paces the hall
back and forth.

INT. CONFERENCE HALL - CONTINUOUS

Council members disagree, agree, and make arguments.

INT. WAITING ROOM AREA - CONTINUOUS

Jusa now enjoys the window view while Duba eats something. Jusa joins Duba to eat.
They don't acknowledge each other.

INT. CONFERENCE HALL - CONTINUOUS

The council members are still trying to make up their minds. Some shake their
heads no, others nods yes. Eventually some no start shrugging their shoulders
maybe. Then finally everyone start nodding yes.

SPEAKER
And does every member of the council,
agree with this decision.

                         EVERYONE
          Yes.

                          SPEAKER
          Well then let us make it official. All who
          agree with this ruling say I.

Everyone nods.

                          EVERYONE
          Aye.

                          SPEAKER
          And all who oppose say nay.

There's silence. The Speaker DRUM again.

                          SPEAKER
          The council has spoken.
                    (to the Guard)
          Escort the Chiefs back inside.

The guard leaves, then returns with the Chiefs. They take their seats on the podium.

                          SPEAKER
          The council has come to a decision, which
          we are satisfied with to be Ma 'at justice
          for everyone involved. And by this ruling
          you will both abide.

Duba and Jusa sit to listen.

                          SPEAKER
          The council of the Kushite Empire has
          ruled that you both have trespassed
          against each other. But because the initial
          violation was by the Mumons the council
          will hold them responsible for provoking
          the conflict.

Jusa stays calm.

                          SPEAKER
          The council's ruling goes as follows, to the
          families of the three kidnapped young
          women, will go a reimbursement by way of

the Mumon's land and gold. The family that lost one daughter will receive twenty-five acres of land, and one hundred pounds of gold. And to the family that lost two daughters, will go fifty acres of land and two hundred pounds of gold for their loss. And to the Aswan tribe as a whole, you Chief Jusa will reimburse them with five thousand pounds of your personal gold. Also the given borders are the same as they were before, so see to it that it is respected. This is the ruling from the council of the Kushite Empire. Which you will-

                    JUSA
This is the council's ruling? And what about the Mumon people, what shall be our justice?

                    SPEAKER
You and your people get your freedom. That is your justice.

                    JUSA
Freedom is our birthright, given to every man by the Ntchru. Where is the Ma 'at justice for all the damages and loss lives that my village was subjected to because of this invasion?

                    SPEAKER
Your people took no loss which was not invited. If your people seek further justice, perhaps you should seek it from the sole survivor of the kidnapers. They are the ones responsible for all of this confusion. Tell the Mumon people to get all the justice that they desire from him. The Council has left him to you and the Mumon people, to do with as you all please.
          (beat)
As I was saying, this is the ruling by the council. Which you will both respect and abide by as seated members of this Kushite Empire. Is this understood?

                    DUBA
Yes it is.

Jusa pauses.

                    SPEAKER
           (to Jusa)
Is this understood?

                     JUSA
           (upset)
Yes it is understood.

                    SPEAKER
The throne will appoint an overseer to
verify that the stipulations are met. That is
all, the council has made its ruling you may
both step down.

Duba and Jusa take their seats with the rest of the council.

                    SPEAKER
At this time I will turn the floor back over
to our honorable host Chief Narmer.

The council applauds. The Speaker steps down. Chief Narmer takes the podium.

                 CHIEF NARMER
Thank you. Once again I would like to
thank each of you for being here today. To
personally see an end to this war between
our brothers the Aswan and the Mumon.
This will only make our Empire stronger.
And us all agreeing to no more war,
between no two villages of this Empire will
only further secure our prosperity.

All the members stand and cheer. Chief Narmer raises his hand to calm them down.

                 CHIEF NARMER
Brothers, brothers, I must take this
opportunity to address a more serious
threat to our empire. A threat that I feel
could destroy the future prosperity of our
Nation, if we the council don't address it.

The threat is the continuous landing of
more and more Foreigners into our Delta
region. Just three weeks ago three more
boats were docked by the Saite leaders,
bringing in more of their countrymen. It is
about time this council face reality. These
invaders have no intention on living up to
the treaty. For too long we have just
looked the other way, letting them do as
they please, as long as they stay out of our
way.

                    POPA
The Foreigners landing have been of no
threat to us. They are only seeking the Nile
Valley experience.

                    CHIEF NARMER
That is your opinion, because your village
does a large percent of your trades with
the Foreigners.

                    POPA
And is that now also a problem?

                    CHIEF NARMER
That is not a problem. But that prohibit
you from seeing the real problem, because
you are too focused on your own personal
gain.

                    POPA
And what is it that I was supposed to have
seen.

                    CHIEF NARMER
History repeating itself. Nothing has
changed with the Foreigners, other than
the borders we have forced them behind.
Their continuous disregard for the treaty
that they signed is more obvious now than
ever before.

                    DUKA
And even with that being true, is that
enough to consider them a threat?

CHIEF NARMER

The Foreigners are always a threat. They have attacked our Empire when we were twice as strong, as we are today. They always have their minds set to conquer. We the leaders of the Empire cannot just sit idly by, and let them continue to land, gaining more strength and numbers.

PRINCE CHALA

I agree with Chief Narmer. These Foreigners continuing to land in the Delta will only continue to push us farther south from the sea coast, cutting us off from some of our most profitable trade routes. I support making them live up to the treaty.

ZOMI

I see no Foreigners looking to conquer us as Chief Narmer claims. The foreign populations of the Kuru village are no conquerors. They abide by, and take part in our traditions as if it were their own. They wouldn't lift a finger against the Empire.

DUKA

The same is true for the foreign population of the Kurgus village. They pose a threat to nobody.

SRCO

You both reside hundreds of miles away from the Delta. The foreign populations in your villages are mostly slaves, or freed slaves with no intentions on rebelling.

ZOMI
(to Chief Narmer)

Since there is a problem with the foreign population of the Delta. What do you suggest we do about them?

CHIEF NARMER

I suggest we give them a proclamation to
live up to their agreement in the treaty. Or
we take back full control of the northern
low lands.

MNFECO

I say we just go and banish them all from
our land. There is no reason to give them a
proclamation. They have been violating
the treaty since the day they agreed to it.

CHIEF NARMER

I agree with Chief Mnfeco, they should not
get a proclamation. But at least with it,
they would see that the camel back has
broken, and that will at least give them the
chance to do right.

RASA

Let us not forget, this is the Foreigners that
we are talking about. They cannot do right.
They know no good, no compromise, no
love.

POPA

It is obvious that there are members of this
council that have become intoxicated with
power.

CHIEF NARMER

The only thing that is obvious is that there
are members of this council, which are not
fit to represent this Kushite Empire. And
you are one of those, you spineless waste
of a man, masquerading around as a
leader.

KING SALO

There is no reason for such remarks. Every
Chief contributes to our Empire's
prosperity. But regardless of who may
disagree with Chief Narmer position. We
must put a stop to this continuous landing
by the Foreigners.

                    POPA
            (upset)
Why don't we just let Narmer handle this
himself, since he is so fit to represent this
Empire.

                CHIEF NARMER
Does the fact that you are not worthy
bothers you.

                    POPA
No Narmer, it is only you that bother me,
you and your attitude as if you always
know what's best for this Empire.

                CHIEF NARMER
Any problem you have with me, I
encourage you to come and please
yourself.

Stare each other down serious.

                  KING SALO
That is enough of this foolishness. Didn't
everyone just moments ago, agree to no
more feuds between ourselves.
            (beat)
Popa regardless of how you may feel about
what Narmer is saying right now. If you
were to recall the history of our Empire,
you will see that a proclamation could only
work out to our benefit.

                    POPA
How could it only work out to our benefit,
when it is liable to restart a war between
the cultures?

                  KING SALO
Confronting the foreign population of the
Delta possibly restarts a war. Overlooking
them continues to weaken our Empire.
Which of the two do you think is in the
best interest of our people?

                    SRCO
I personally have no problem with the
Foreigners, but I am at Khem with a
firsthand view and witness there
population increase every season. They
aren't subversive at the moment but who
knows how long that will last for.

                    ZOMI
You see the problem, but still you have no
problem with the Aliens. Which is it, are
they a problem, or aren't they?

                    SRCO
Certainly they are a problem, didn't I just
state their population increase every
season. How could an increasing foreign
population not be a problem to the
Empire?

                 CHIEF NARMER
Since there are so many mixed feelings
about this issue. I will remove this burden
from the rest of the council. I will take
Popa's advice and make this problem mine
alone.

The council sits shocked.

                 CHIEF NARMER
I will personally go and address the
foreign population of the Delta. I will go
and give them the proclamation, and see to
it that this time they abide by it. Once
again thank you all for coming, I trust you
all know your way out...

Chief Narmer walks out, leaving the council members shocked. Djer stands to defend
his father.

                    DJER
How dare, members of this council sit
here, and question the intentions of my
father. My ancestors including my father
have done more for this Empire than any
of you sitting here. And now you all, his

fellow Council members react as if he
speaks with personal motives. What my
father just stated is certainly true. There
are members of this Council that is not
worthy to represent this Empire.
              (to Popa)
You all are not even worthy to consider
yourselves natives of your own country...

Djer walks out, leaving the council members as well.

                    MNFECO
              (sarcastically)
Well there is no doubt he is his father's
son. I for one support Chief Narmer and
will stand with him every step of the way.

Mnfeco leaves as well.

                    DUBA
              (stands)
I too support Chief Narmer's decision, and
will assist him in any way I can.

He leaves.

                    POPA
              (stands)
I see no threat from the foreigners, and
will take no part in revolting against them
until I see ample reason to do so.

He leaves.

                    JUSA
              (stands)
My tribe is in the midst of our own crisis,
and do not have the peace of mind to take
part in any of this.

All the members of the council walk out.

INT. GUEST AREA - CONTINUOUS

Chief Narmer and Djer are talking with Mnfeco when some other members of the
Council walk in.

                    MNFECO
Even though it is perfectly clear where I
stand on this issue. Nonetheless I couldn't
leave here today without emphasizing
once more. Whenever the time comes to
take action, please do not hesitate to call
on me. I support you, and pledge to stand
with you every step of the way.

                CHIEF NARMER
I thank you for your support my brother.
Because when that time does come, the
help of you and the Hierak warriors will be
greatly needed and appreciated.

                    MNFECO
We are more than happy to do our duty.
Once again, my apologies for the way the
meeting ended, you were a gracious host.

Duba enters, and walks toward Chief Narmer.

                CHIEF NARMER
            (nods)
Thank you. But perhaps I should be
apologizing to you.

                    MNFECO
There is no wrong, in defending your
nation. And I aim to be the living testimony
of this statement.

                CHIEF NARMER
Well my brother I say to you, and the
Hierak warriors ready yourselves, and
keep an ear out for my word. For your wait
to live and prove could be short.

                    MNFECO
            (bows)
You could depend on us. Until that time!

                CHIEF NARMER
            (bows)
Until that time.

Mnfeco leaves. Duba walks up. They nod to each other in respect while passing.

                    DUBA
              (bows)
          You stormed out, before I got a chance to
          thank you.

                    CHIEF NARMER
          There is no reason to thank me.

                    DUBA
          The people of Aswan and I would say
          different, if we had anything to say about
          it. So on behalf of the entire Aswan village,
          I would like to say thank you, for gathering
          all the members of the council here today
          and putting an end to the war between my
          people and the Mumons. Also I would like
          to assure you, that all of the Aswan
          warriors are at your disposal, in any action
          you decide to take towards the Delta.

                    CHIEF NARMER
          Your Empire thanks you. The Aswan
          support will certainly be appreciated.

Zomi walks in the room and heads toward Chief Narmer.

                    DUBA
          Do not think twice to ask.

He bows to Chief Narmer.

                    DUBA
          It was good seeing you again as usual old
          friend.

                    CHIEF NARMER
              (bows back)
          And the same to you my friend.

                    DUBA
          Once again. Thank you.

Duba leaves. Zomi walks up. They nod respectfully in passing. Zomi then bows to Narmer.

                    ZOMI
          There was no reason to walk out on the
          meeting.

                    CHIEF NARMER
          A meeting not getting anywhere is always
          a reason to walk out.

                    ZOMI
          Is that so. I thought debating, and
          everyone shearing their opinion, was the
          process of a meeting.

                    CHIEF NARMER
          Yes, debating, and shearing opinions. Not
          everyone disagreeing. That was just a
          waste of my time talking to waste men.
          How could a leader disagree with
          protecting themselves and their people
          from a potential threat?

                    ZOMI
          Never mind that, despite all the
          disagreeing, I for one support you in any
          decision you make.

                    CHIEF NARMER
          I thank you. I am grateful to hear that.

They bow to each other.

                    ZOMI
          There is no need to thank me. It's like you
          said it is our duty. Until that time, Huh.

                    CHIEF NARMER
                 (nods)
          Until that time.

Zomi leaves, King Salo enters the room with Prince Chala, Srco, Rasa, and Bobo.
Zomi nods in respect while passing them.

The King notices Berenib in the room. They greet each other. Prince Chala, Sico, Rasa, and Bobo go address Chief Narmer.

                    BERENIB
               (kneels)
          My dare King Salo. I welcome you to our
          home once again.

                    KING SALO
          The ever-lovely Berenib. I see you're still
          as glorious as ever. It's good to see you
          again. How have you been doing?

                    BERENIB
          I have been good. And how about yourself,
          have you been taking life easy.

                    KING SALO
          Easy is the only way I could take it these
          days.

                    BERENIB
          It seems to be working for you. You are
          still going strong. How is the Queen?

                    KING SALO
          She is good, still as beautiful as ever. Still
          putting up with me. How are the children?

                    BERENIB
          They are all well.

                    KING SALO
          That is good, you and Narmer should be
          very proud. Young Djer made a speech
          today at the meeting of the council
          defending his father. And I must personally
          tell you, that fruit did not fall far from the
          tree.

                    BERENIB
               (surprised)
          Really now.

KING SALO
Yes. And if your other children grow to be
as conscious as Djer, you might have given
birth to the future leaders of the Kushite
Empire.

BERENIB
Well that is something that I as a mother
would love to see come to pass.

KING SALO
Did Narmer mention to you that he came
to visit me three weeks ago?

BERENIB
Ahh, yes he did.

KING SALO
Did he also tell you that I once again, asked
him to be my successor?

BERENIB
Ahh, as a matter of fact, no not this time.
No he did not.

KING SALO
Oh, but you have heard of me asking in the
pass?

BERENIB
Yes, he has mentioned it in the pass.

KING SALO
Okay, good. You must clarify something for
me, because I am confused. Am I wrong for
thinking he deserves the position?

BERENIB
No, not at all my King. Both you and I along
with the majority of the Empire thinks that
you are attempting to make a wise choice.

KING SALO
But for some reason beyond me, your
husband does not seem to think so.

Chief Narmer shakes hands with Prince Chala, Srco, Rasa, and Dobo. They all bow in respect and leave. Chief Narmer heads toward his wife and the King.

                    KING SALO
          Perhaps you could help me. I need to find
          some kind of way to convince your
          husband to accept the position.

                    BERENIB
          What do you have in mind?

                    KING SALO
          Nothing in particular, but something must
          be done.
                    (beat)
          The truth be told, I have no other
          candidate for successor in mind, or even
          someone that comes close.

                    BERENIB
          In situations such as this my King, you
          must keep at least two, or three options.

                    KING SALO
          Trust me Berenib I am aware of that, but it
          is hard to keep options, when no one else
          measures up to Chief Narmer.

                    BERENIB
          I will see what I could do.

                    CHIEF NARMER
                    (walks up, and bow)
          Old man, what have I told you about
          wooing my wife?

                    KING SALO
          You 're lucky that I am an old man, or else I
          would be given you a run for your Jewel.

                    CHIEF NARMER
          Old man not even in your prime, you still
          would not have stood a chance.

                    KING SALO
You wish. Come let us talk about the issues
you left in limbo earlier.

Chief Narmer kisses his wife on the cheek.

                 CHIEF NARMER
My love pardon us for a moment.

                    BERENIB
Sure. My King it was an honor seeing you
again. And I will see what I could do about
that for you.

                    KING SALO
Thank you, I would greatly appreciate it. It
was good seeing you again also.
          (to Berenib)
Until next time, continue to take good care
of yourself.

                    BERENIB
          (bows)
I will my King. Thank you.

                 CHIEF NARMER
What was that all about.

                    KING SALO
Never mind that. What was that all about
earlier? You of all people should know that
is not the way to get your point across at a
council meeting.

                 CHIEF NARMER
I know my King. I just could not go on
arguing about something, I personally feel
that no member of this Council should
have to think twice about.

                    KING SALO
That is true. None of the members should
have to think twice about it, but not
everyone is going to shear your point of
view.

                    CHIEF NARMER
I realize that. But I do expect them to see
themselves in the grand scale of life. I do
expect them to be able to recognize a
friend from a foe. Them being members of
this council, which is directly responsible
for the welfare of the people of this
Empire, I need to feel secure in their
thought process and decision making.

                    KING SALO
I have told you before, not everyone could
recognize a potential problem. And even if
they could, not everyone will care enough
to do something about it.
          (beat)
But never you mind that, I do not want you
to feel as if it is all left up to you alone to
do something about this situation. I want
you to know that the throne and I, are
behind you one hundred percent. Any
action you decide to take, it will be an
honor to take it with you. So do not
hesitate to call on me.

                    CHIEF NARMER
I thank you my King, your support means
everything to me. I will keep you updated
on our progress. And if the time comes
when we need to take action, the throne
and the Kings Madjai warriors will be the
first ones called upon.

                    KING SALO
Just you say the word, and I will have the
Madjai warriors there to assist you.

They shake hands.

                    CHIEF NARMER
          (bows)
Your loyalty to your Empire is truly
appreciated, I could not ask for more.

                         KING SALO
Did you hear of the speech Djer made
today defending you, after you walked out
of the meeting.

                      CHIEF NARMER
                       (surprised)
Djer made a speech? I heard nothing of it.
What did he say?

                         KING SALO
It's the stuff legends are made of. After you
left he stood up and.....

Chief Narmer confronts Djer.

                      CHIEF NARMER
I heard of the speech you made today at
the end of the meeting.

                           DJER
My apologizes father, I meant no
disrespect.

                      CHIEF NARMER
No my son, you have done nothing wrong
to apologize for. As a matter of fact, I am
very proud of you.

                           DJER
                       (surprised)
You are?

                      CHIEF NARMER
Certainly. Its not everyday a father hears
for the first time, how his first born son
stands in the midst of the members of the
council, to defend his father's point of
view.

                           DJER
It was more than just defending you. This
just so happen to be an issue, on which we
shear the same perspective.

CHIEF NARMER
Really, I had no idea you had a perspective
on issues pertaining to this Empire.

DJER
Not initially, but while sitting in a meeting,
and hearing an issue addressed. I like
everyone else form an opinion about how I
think the issue should be handled.

CHIEF NARMER
That is the process. It sounds as if you are
coming of age, as if its time to appoint you
to a position of responsibility.

DJER
Do you really think I am ready father? I am
only fifteen years of age!

CHIEF NARMER
Sure you are ready. By age seventeen I was
already a governor of the Nekheb village.
By the age of twenty-four I was Chief.
Appointing you to a position of
responsibility will allow you to see if your
decision making, are beneficial to others. It
will further prepare you for your future.

DJER
If you think the time is right, it would be
my pleasure, and honor to serve my village
and my Empire. What position do you have
in mind?

CHIEF NARMER
(proudly)
I think I will start you off in agriculture
first. How about assistant supervisor, to
oversee the needs of the tillers, and to
weigh what they reap each harvest. Then
make sure it is evenly distributed to the
people of the village and the remaining
stored away for the drought seasons.

DJER

I know nothing about farming. How about something in artillery manufacturing or combat training?

CHIEF NARMER

That will all come in due time. But agriculture is where I will have you start. It is the foundation on which strong nations are built. It is the first lesson one should learn when learning to govern. The basic welfare of a people, depend on their leader's ability to provide provision for them. Plus it is a process which will bring you closer to the Ntchru. It will help you to better understand, and appreciate the beauty in the experience which is life. True knowing your artillery and combat training are all a part of being a strong leader. But you are already being taught the two and have been since the age of five. It is now time for the next phase of your rights of passage, to further prepare you to be a true leader one day. There is nothing more fulfilling to a true leader, than to see a seed that he have planted, grow and bear its fruits so that him and his people could eat from it and sustain themselves. It allows you to be the creator, even though you have no real control over the process. It is not like brick masonry where you sculpt and shape, as you will. Or painting a portrait, where you gather your brushes and colors, and do as you feel fit. Agriculture makes man humble himself, watch life manifest, and ponder the mysteries this Universe holds. At best the most man could do is plant the seed and add water, if it grows and bears its fruits, it did so by a will much greater than man. Through this process of creation, I personally have come to understand the power of the Ntchru who are our Creators, Providers and Saviors. It is like Ra leaving every night, but returning every morning. These events my son, are willed by a energy much greater than man. This being your first post of responsibility, I know it will allow you to know yourself, while teaching you how to provide and address the needs of others.

                    DJER
Father if you feel that passionate about it.
It would be my honor and pleasure to take
this position.

Chief Narmer shakes his son's hand proudly.

                CHIEF NARMER
Then my son it is yours. I just ask that you
live up to the family name.

                    DJER
                (anxiously)
I promise you. I will do my best to do so.

                CHIEF NARMER
I am very proud of you my son.

                    DJER
Thank you father.

Chief Narmer claps his hands.

                CHIEF NARMER
Everyone. Everyone could I have your
attention. Everyone please gather around.

Everyone goes silent.

                CHIEF NARMER
I Chief Narmer have just appointed my
first born son Djer, as assistant supervisor
of agriculture. In charge of overseeing the
needs of the farmers, also in charge of the
weighing, distributing, and storing of
Nekheb's yearly harvest.

Everyone applauds. Djer raises his hand and nods. Berenib claps proudly as various
people walk over to congratulate Djer. Fusa approaches him.

                    FUSA
Congratulations to you Djer, it was full
time now that you were assigned a post of
responsibility. You are now well on your
way to becoming a man.

                    DJER
Thank you. It has been a long time coming,
and now finally I have been assigned a
position, a rank, and a title.

                    FUSA
Make good on this opportunity and you
may very well one day become Chief.

                    DJER
That's my intentions.

Fusa nods, then turns to leave when Chief Narmer stops him. They step to the side to
talk.

                    CHIEF NARMER
I want you to round up a posse of two
hundred warriors, ready to ride out at first
light. I am going to pay a visit to the
foreign population of the Delta.

                    FUSA
Right away my Chief.

Fusa leaves. Chief Narmer walks over to Berenib, they stand together and watch
Djer proudly. The guests eventually begin to exit and leave for home.

INT. NARMER'S PALACE - BEDROOM - NIGHT

Chief Narmer and his family retire to their quarters. Chief Narmer and Berenib are
intimate all night. Both of them are in love's bliss throughout the night.

INT. NARMER'S PALACE - DAY

Chief Narmer wakes up and prepares to leave. Berenib sees Narmer off.

EXT. NARMER'S PALACE - DAY

Chief Narmer goes outside to meet his posse, including Fusa. They mount their
horses and ride out.

EXT. NEKHEB TOWN - DAY

They ride through the town. A few stalls are open with others just opening up. The
OWNERS remove their shop covers.

LOCALS arrive in town. Everyone watches as Chief Narmer and his posse go through, sensing something is about to happen.

EXT. NILE RIVER - DAY

The posse rides their horses onto awaiting boats docked on the Nile. The sun shines brightly as Narmer and posse sail to their first stop in the Delta.

EXT. ATHRA - DAY

The boats dock at Athra. Chief Narmer and his posse mount their horses and ride off into the nearby village. As they ride through, RESIDENTS tense up.

TWO HUNDRED KUSHITE WARRIORS ride through their town. The posse stops at the local leader's residence.

                    CHIEF NARMER
          I'm here to see Donoe.

                    D GUARD
          Very well Chief Narmer, I will alert him at
          once.

The guard goes inside.

INT. DONOE'S HOUSE - DAY

DONOE is speaking with SOMEONE.

                    D GUARD
          Pardon me sir, Chief Narmer is here
          requesting to see you.

                    DONOE
               (surprised)
          Chief Narmer is here to see me? I wonder
          what could this be about.

Donoe gets up and goes outside to greet Narmer.

EXT. DONOE'S HOUSE - CONTINUOUS

When Donoe gets outside, he's surprised to see the army of warriors behind Chief Narmer.

                    DONOE
Chief Narmer. This is an overwhelming
surprise. Please come in.

Chief Narmer gets off his horse and goes inside. Fusa follows him.

INT. DONOE'S HOUSE - CONTINUOUS

                    DONOE
Honorable Chief, please make yourselves
comfortable.

Narmer takes a seat.

                 CHIEF NARMER
Three weeks ago, three more boats docked
in the Delta. Were you in any way involved
with those landings?

                    DONOE
Oh, no Chief, not at all.

                 CHIEF NARMER
Would you happen to know who is
responsible for the landings?

                    DONOE
No I do not Chief. I only know of the
landings, because it was the night the
warrior's victory drums sounded. As it
sounded I was awoken, at which time I
stepped out for a breath of fresh air, and
noticed the docking's in the distance.

                 CHIEF NARMER
And what about new faces in the
community, have you noticed any new
residents?

                    DONOE
No Chief, I have not notice any.

                 CHIEF NARMER
It really does not matter anyway, because
such actions are now just privileges of the
pass. From this day forth until stated

otherwise, the Kushite Empire will no
longer tolerate the smuggling in of illegal
aliens.

                    DONOE
If I may ask, why do the Chief bring such
proclamation to me? As if I am a smuggler.

                  CHIEF NARMER
I am not telling you this with the slightest
concern, of if you are a smuggler. I am
telling you this because if the landings
continue, you and every other Foreigner in
the Delta will face the same consequences.
So make mention to each and every
Foreigner you come across far and wide.
The treaty was signed, and it will be
honored. I suggest you advise the Delta to
live up to it. Any further smuggling in of
illegal aliens will immediately result in the
Empire taking back full control of the Delta
regions. And forbid every Foreigner, from
operating freely.

                    DONOE
                  (surprised)
Forbid Foreigners from operating freely in
the Delta. The majority of the Foreigners in
the Delta like myself, are not involve in, or
know anything of the smuggling in of any
aliens. Such drastic actions by the Empire
would be unfair to the majority of us.

                  CHIEF NARMER
                    (upset)
Unfair. This continuous violation of the
treaty, that's what's unfair. And you
Foreigners just continue to do so with no
regards for us the natives of this land. But
as I have just stated, such days have ended.

Chief Narmer ends the conversation there. He gets up and leaves. Donoe can tell
Narmer is upset. Donoe sits pondering.

EXT. DONOE'S HOUSE - CONTINUOUS

Chief Narmer mounts his horse. His posse and him ride back to the Nile, and get back onto their waiting boats.

INT. BEN'S HOUSE - DAY

Srtife and Lena make pottery.

> LENA
> It is quite easy you just slide your hands over it, and mold it into the shape you wish.

> SRTIFE
> It doesn't seem to be working for me.

His clay pot falls apart.

> LENA
> Come let me show you once again.

She takes his hands and they mold the clay together.

> SRTIFE
> This way is much better. It always turns out perfect when we do it together.

Lena looks up. They get distracted stare into each other eyes. The sculpture suddenly collapses again.

Blossom enters and calls Lena.

> BLOSSOM
> Lena.
> (beat)
> Lena!

Lena cleans off the clay.

> LENA
> Yes Ma'am.

> BLOSSOM
> Come here for a moment darling, I need you to go to the market for me.

                    LENA
          Okay. Coming mother.
                (to Srtife)
          Are you going to accompany me to the
          market.

                    SRTIFE
          I 'm not sure. Will that be wise?

                    LENA
          Sure. New faces arrive in the village all the
          time. Besides, you have got to get to know
          the town sooner or later.

Lena gets a bucket, and removes a plug. Water runs out and she washes her hands.
She goes to the kitchen where Blossom and Ann are cooking.

                    LENA
                (to Blossom)
          What is it that you need from the market
          mother?

                    BLOSSOM
                (hands her gold)
          Go to the butcher shop for me, and buy ten
          pounds of freshly killed lamb.

                    LENA
          Okay Ma'am.

She walks toward the gate. Srtife sneaks up behind her and puts his hand over her
eyes.

                    SRTIFE
          Guess who.

                    LENA
          Hopefully my companion to the market.

                    SRTIFE
          Lucky for you it is.

EXT. BUBA - DAY

Chief Narmer and his posse arrive and dock their boats at Buba. They mount their horses and ride off into the village. The LOCALS are shocked just like they were in the last town. They stop to watch the posse ride through.

INT. BUTCHER SHOP - DAY

Lena and Srtife buys meat at the butcher shop.

                    MEAT MAN
          Ten pounds of lamb you say?

                    LENA
          Yes sir, ten pounds.

                    MEAT MAN
               (measures the meat)
          Okay, here you go. So how are your
          parents?

He hands the meat to her. She gives him the gold.

                    LENA
          They are doing good.

                    MEAT MAN
          And who is your friend?

                    LENA
          This is Srtife, the son of a friend of my
          father. He is from further south at Khem.

                    MEAT MAN
          Oh, okay.
               (to Srtife)
          Good to meet you Srtife, is this your first
          time in Buba.

He shakes his hand.

                    SRTIFE
          Ah, yes it is actually.

                    MEAT MAN
          You will find it is very peaceful here in
          Buba, no one to bother you.

                         SRTIFE
So I have heard.

Srtife smirks.

                         MEAT MAN
You take care, my friend.
            (to Lena)
And Lena you give your parents my
regards.

                         LENA
I will sir, and you have a good day.

As they turn to leave, the first set of Warriors on horses go by. They all stand shocked by what they see outside. They go out to get a closer look.

EXT. BUTCHER SHOP - DAY

They stand in shock.

INT. BAR - DAY

Jaugen is siting in a bar a couple stalls down from the butcher shop when the first round of Warriors go by. He goes outside to see what's happening. When he gets outside he sees Chief Narmer and his posse ride by.

EXT. STING'S HOUSE - DAY

Chief Narmer and his posse address S GUARD outside the house. The Guard goes inside and comes back with STING.

                         STING
       Come inside.

Narmer and Fusa follows sting inside.

INT. STING'S HOUSE - CONTINUOUS

                         STING
So Chief Narmer, if I may ask. What is it
that has brought you to Buba in such
numbers?

CHIEF NARMER

I am making my rounds in the Delta, and this is one of my stops. Three more boats docked in the Delta three weeks ago, and I am here to address it.

STING

Oh I see. I have heard about the recent dockings.

CHIEF NARMER

What is happening up here in the Delta? Don't you and the other residents have any intentions on stopping the Saite leaders, ongoing practice of importing their foreign countrymen into your native land?

STING

They operate in secrecy, under the shadow of night. There is no real way of knowing when it is going to happen, which makes it that much harder to prevent.

CHIEF NARMER

Everybody who is anybody knows there are no secrets in the Delta.
        (beat)
True, you all come from the loins of these foreign men, but your mothers are as native as the rich black soil of Kush. This is where the Goddess gave birth to you. Kush is your birthright, and why you Mulattos keep giving it to the Foreigners is beyond me.

STING

You speak as if the Mulattos invited them here. The new comers in the Delta function as a community supporting each other. I know nothing about their landings. They no longer need assistance from outsiders to execute a plan and meet their objective.

CHIEF NARMER
The new comers becoming self reliant, is
no reason to not know what is going on
around you.

STING
There are more Kushites in the Delta than
any other strain of people. Why didn't the
Kushites find out about the landings, and
warn the Empire.

CHIEF NARMER
This is why I ask, what is happening in the
Delta. It is as if all the occupants think
that you all are an island and has no one
to answer to.

STING
Oh no Chief Narmer, that is never the
case. The Buban residents and I have the
highest of respect, and honor for the laws
and constitutions of the Kushite Empire.

CHIEF NARMER
You and the Bubans only respect and
honor the laws and constitutions, which
allows you all to go unchecked. But as of
today I personally will give you
something that I assure you, the entire
Delta will respect and honor.

EXT. BUBA VILLAGE - DAY

Lena and Srtife stands in the CROWD watching. They're talking with each other
when a hand reaches from behind and grab Srtife on his shoulder, scaring him.
It's Jaugen.

SRTIFE
(to Jaugen)
You frightened the crap out of me.

JAUGEN
This is not the place you should be right
now.

SRTIFE

I am simply trying to observe the Kushites
to find out what is going on.

JAUGEN

You could very well, be what's going on.
But here and now is not the place or time
to find out.

LENA
(to Srtife)
That is exactly what I am thinking. Let us
get out of here.

Srtife and Lena leaves. Jaugen stays to keep an eye on what's going on.

INT. STING'S HOUSE - DAY

STING
(pleads)
What do you mean take back full control
of all the Delta regions? I could
understand the Empire restricting the
Foreigners, and holding them responsible
for their actions. But the Mulatto
community knew nothing of, and had
nothing to do with their activities.

CHIEF NARMER

And there lies the problem, how could you
govern an area, and know nothing about
the activities the residents practice on a
regularly basis. That only leaves me to
assume that you the leader either know,
and profit from it, so you do nothing to
stop it. Or your village limits stretches
further than your arms length, and this
problem is much further than your spear
can reach.
(beat)
Either way this Empire cannot endure the
incompetence.

STING

Let us not forget the Empire currently and
have always controlled the Delta regions.

If it is out of my reach, why haven't the
Empire stepped in and prevented the
ongoing landings.

> CHIEF NARMER
> That is exactly why the Empire is taking
> this stance now. I advise you to spread
> the word.

Chief narmer stands to leave. Sting stands as well.

> STING
> Please. Chief Narmer I beg of you, to
> please ask the Council to consider the
> majority of the Delta population, whom
> has nothing to do with the landings.

> CHIEF NARMER
> We have. This is why the Delta gets one
> last chance to live up to the treaty. Now if
> you will pardon me, I must be on my way.

Narmer and his posse leave Sting standing there. Sting enraged smashes his
drinking mug against the wall.

EXT. STING'S HOUSE - CONTINUOUS

The entire community stands watching, including Jaugen, who makes his way
through the crowd. He recognizes Chief Narmer.

Sting walks out onto his balcony, which overlooks the community. Sting addresses
his people.

> STING
> (shouts angrily)
> People of Buba lend me your ears.

They all listen intently.

> STING
> As you all could see, we have just been
> visited by Chief Narmer. Chief Narmer has
> left all the way from Nekheb to come here
> and tell us that, the three boats that landed
> three weeks ago, even though we might

not have had anything to do with it, the
Empire is still holding us all responsible.

The crowd erupts in anger.

                    CROWD
                   (various)
     Hah what? That is crazy. I own no boats.
     What did he say? That is injustice. I had
     nothing to do with it.

                    STING
     Yes that's right. You all heard me
     correctly, holding us all responsible.

The crowd continues to go crazy.

                    CROWD
                   (various)
     This is not fair. The docking is not my
     doing. I know nothing about sailing the sea.

                    STING
     But that is not all, Chief Narmer also said
     if any other unauthorized landing is to
     take place. The Empire will take back full
     control of the entire Delta region,
     forbidding us from operating freely.

The crowd ROARS.

                    CROWD
     But we have nothing to do with the
     landings. We will never let that happen.
     This is injustice. Over our dead bodies!
     They will never take back the Delta. But
     we had nothing to do with the landings.
     Let them come and try to take it back.

Jaugen listens from the crowd. Chief Narmer and his posse hear the ROARING from a
distance.

                    FUSA
                   (to Narmer)
     What do you suppose that's all about?

                    CHIEF NARMER
          That is the sound of boys starting to grow
          hair around their testicles, so now they
          feel as if they are men. But we will soon
          see how much of a man they are.

Sting stands on his balcony, watching Chief Narmer and his posse in the distance.

                        STING
                      (shouts)
          Do you hear that Narmer? You take that
          back to your Empire.

Sting and the entire Buban community watch Chief Narmer and his posse leave. They shout their disapproval at Narmer. Jaugen leaves for home to inform Ben.

EXT. NILE RIVER- CONTINUOUS

Chief Narmer and his posse get back on the boats, and dismount off their horses once again.

EXT. SAIS VILLAGE - DAY

Chief Narmer and his posse arrive at the docks of Sais. They dock their boats, go on land and ride toward the town.

Once again, the locals all watch as the posse pass through. They stop outside of Beirut's house. Narmer stays on his horse with his warriors around him.

                    CHIEF NARMER
          This is very nice. It looks as if life has been
          very prosperous for you both here in the
          Delta.

                        BEIRUT
          Well I often hear that us Foreigners only
          get one life to live so I try to enjoy it. I
          must say this is a very overwhelming
          surprise, may I ask what brings you to
          Sais in such numbers.

                    CHIEF NARMER
          Just the two most powerful men in the
          entire Delta.

BEIRUT
(sarcastically)
And your expedition led you here. You
must have made a wrong turn somewhere
along your way.

CHIEF NARMER
I have made no wrong turns. I am here to
address the latest landings from three
weeks ago. And all proficiency points to
you two.

KALILI
(from the balcony)
And what exactly makes all proficiency
point to us.

CHIEF NARMER
Everyone knows not even a grain of spice
could be moved to or from the Delta,
without you two knowing about it.

The crowd moves in closer to watch.

KALILI
(sarcastically)
You Kushites are the giants amongst man,
the ones who see, hear, and know the
mysteries of the Universe. Not us.

CHIEF NARMER
That story sound very embracing, very
soothing, but tell it to someone who is
sympathetic to your existence. I am here
representing the Empire to assure you all
that, the giant have awaken. And any
smuggling in of aliens, from here on is
strictly forbidden.

BEIRUT
And why do you warn us, we have no
knowledge of navigating the sea?

CHIEF NARMER
Perhaps not, but you do know and have
extreme influence, over many men that

does. The practice of alien smuggling is strictly forbidden. No one should know that better than you two.

                    BEIRUT
You are correct Chief Narmer we do know that it is forbidden. That is why we take part in no such activity. We respect the laws of the land.

                 CHIEF NARMER
Well since you all are such law abiding, residents. I suggest you both teach the other Foreigners of the Delta to do the same. Because if there are any further landings. The entire population of the Delta will be held accountable.

                    BEIRUT
We sympathize with the Kushite natives, but surely we all cannot be held accountable for the actions of a few men, who break the agreement of the treaty.

                 CHIEF NARMER
Yes, you all could. And from this day forth you all will.

The crowd starts mumbling.

                    CROWD
That is not reasonable. How could this be?

                    KALILI
Pardon me Chief Narmer, perhaps it is just me. But it seems as if the council has been part taking in some heavy drinking, or you all are just drunk with power.

Chief Narmer doesn't like that.

                 CHIEF NARMER
Any further landings of any illegal Aliens in the Delta from here on, will immediately result in the Empire taking back full control of the Delta.

The crowd erupts.

                                CROWD
                    This is injustice. What is the meaning of
                    all this? We will not stand for this. What is
                    going on here? We have done nothing
                    wrong.

The crowd ROARS with anger and resentment. THREE CROWD MEMBERS charge
Chief Narmer.

                              SAIS REBELS
                    Ahhh, the giant was slain during It's
                    slumber. You will have to bring the
                    depths of Kemet to take back the Delta.

                                BEIRUT
                    Noooo.

Beirut tries to stop them, but regardless they draw their swords in anger and charge
Chief Narmer.

The Kushite Warriors cock their bows, TWO shooters shoot, and kills two of the
charging rebels. The other Kushite Warriors take aim at the rest of the compound
while Narmer takes out his spear.

Narmer throws his spear directly into the chest of the last charging Rebel.

The crowd stops Roaring, and Beirut stops screaming.

Chief Narmer rides over and plucks his spear out of the rebel's chest. The Kushite
Warriors still aiming their bows at the entire compound. Chief Narmer holds his
bloody spear in his hand and says.

                             CHIEF NARMER
                    As I have just stated, any further landings
                    of illegal aliens in the Delta, will result in
                    the Empire taking back full control of the
                    Delta regions, no longer allowing you all
                    to operate freely. Now is there anyone
                    else amongst you all who do not
                    comprehend what I have just stated.

He looks around.

                    CHIEF NARMER
          Anyone? Be it a leader or a resident of the
          community. Good, because you all will be
          held accountable. The Kushite Empire has
          spoken.

Chief Narmer starts riding out. His posse rides out behind him in sequence, making
sure he's covered at all times.

They exit the compound onto the street. The locals are still watching. They head
back to the Nile River.

Beirut stands watching. He signals to his GUARDS to remove the dead bodies. The
crowd is still filled with unrest, talking with each other. Kalili steps forward and
address them.

                    KALILI
          People of Sais, I ask you to please
          compose yourself. We are a hard working,
          law-abiding community trying to make a
          better life for ourselves. I, like the rest of
          you are not responsible for, nor do we
          know anything of any boats docking. So to
          the Kushites who think they could take
          our privileges unjustly, without a fight, I
          say over my dead body.

The crowd erupts.

                    CROWD
          Ya over my dead body. Damn the
          Kushites. We want justice.

                    KALILI
          In these times, we know not what these
          Kushites are thinking. So to every man I
          say, continue to obey there laws, but be
          ready at all times to defend yourself, and
          your fellow man that stands with you. For
          in these times of uncertainty, only a true
          comrade will stand with you.

The crowd cheers.

KALILI

And as I stand here before you, I give my
word to you all. I will give my last breath
before I stand aside, and let the Kushites
injustice get the best of us.

The crowd erupts, with cheers, and praises for Kalili as he looks at them. Beirut
makes his way through the crowd, over to Kalili.

BEIRUT
(sinisterly)
It seems as if our trespasses have led the
Kushites to wrath.

KALILI
Perfect, exactly what we have been
hoping for, a way to push their hand
forcing an all out war.

BEIRUT
Are you sure now is the right time. At the
moment it seems as if the entire Empire is
with one accord.

KALILI
The Empire as a whole could never be with
one accord. There is always an odd man
out. The timing is perfect, just as our
trained fighters in the old country, are
gaining remarkable strength and numbers.
Us with reinforcement the Kushites know
nothing about and them with a declining
Empire we know everything about. My
friend the timing could not be better, the
Universe has turned in our favor. All we
need to do now is to have the locals of the
Delta cry injustice. Declaring they have
nothing to do with the landings. To push
the wedge further between the Empire
different Chiefs and the different opinions
on how this matter should be handled.

BEIRUT
Only if the Mumons were not in captivity, we
would still have a strong ally in the Empire.

                        KALILI
            Never mind that, we still have a good
            relationship with the Kurus, the Kurgus,
            and the Kermans. Contact them all and find
            out how they feel about the council's cruel,
            unjust ruling. And contact Sting also. Find
            out how they feel about the Mulattos
            freedom being threatened. As for me, I will
            visit the villages in the north. But most
            importantly, I will get message to the
            fighters in the old country. Letting them
            know that our time has come.

They nod to eachother. Beirut leaves to go secure his allies.

EXT. BOATS ON RIVER - DAY

Chief Narmer and his posse on boats headed to the next village. All the Nekheb
warriors are relaxing and eating when they arrive at the dock.

The locals watch curiously as the Nekheb warriors rides through their town, and
heads to the local leader's residence.

EXT. KWAME'S HOUSE - DAY

Chief Narmer and his warriors arrive outside the house of Kwame. Narmer address
the Guard who leads him inside to talk with Kwame.

INT. KWAME'S HOUSE - DAY

                    CHIEF NARMER
                    (to Kwame)
            I 'm here to address the recent landings.

                    KWAME
            I had nothing to do with it.

                    CHIEF NARMER
            That is probably true, but on this issue, it
            does not matter.

He gets up to leave, shakes Kwame's hand. They leave Kwame standing with a
worried look on his face.

EXT. KWAME'S HOUSE - CONTINUOUS

Chief Narmer and his posse mount their horses and ride back through town. They get back to the Nile River, board their boats, and sail to the next village.

EXT. RUMAH VILLAGE - DAY

Chief Narmer and his warriors reach the Village of Rumah. They ride through the town and head straight to the local leaders residence.

EXT. RAH'S HOUSE - DAY

Narmer address the GUARD standing at the gate. The guard goes inside and comes back with Rah.

> RAH
> Come inside.

Narmer and Fusa follow Rah inside.

INT. RAH'S HOUSE - DAY

> CHIEF NARMER
> No more illegal boat dockings.

> RAH
> But Chief, I 'm innocent of it.

They leave, mount their horses, and head back to the Nile River where they board their boats again. This time, they are headed back home to Nekheb.

INT. BOAT - NIGHT

Fusa walks up to Narmer, who is gazing into space.

> FUSA
> This campaign was very fulfilling.
> Addressing the people of the Delta, to put
> an end to the landings was absolutely an
> essential action.

> CHIEF NARMER
> Fulfilling it was, but from here on is where
> the real campaign will begin. The foreign
> population of the Delta are too defiant, to
> let a proclamation change their motives. I

want you to keep an extra ear on the
ground to hear every step the foreign
population makes from here on. Because I
am determined to be the thorn that drives
through there foot, the next time they take
a wrong step.

Fusa nods. The boats sail into the night.

EXT. NEKHEB VILLAGE - NIGHT

The entire group gets off the boats, gets on their horses, and heads their separate
ways.

INT. NARMER'S PALACE - NIGHT

Chief Narmer walks into his bedroom where Berenib helps him remove his armor.

EXT. SAIS VILLAGE - DAY

Beirut and his COMPANY mount horses and ride out.

EXT. BUBA VILLAGE - DAY

Beirut and his Company reach the first village.

INT. BEN'S HOUSE - DAY

Ann stands over pots shearing food when Ben walks into the kitchen.

                         ANN
             Good morning darling, I have your
             breakfast and tea prepared for you.

                         BEN
             I have no time to eat this morning.

He kisses her cheek and takes a bite.

                         BEN
             I'm on my way to town.

Alsi overhears.

                         ALSI
             Could I accompany you to town?

                    BEN
With everything that is going on, it is best
to avoid the town until things calm down.
I won't be long. I am only going to hear
the length of what took place yesterday.

                    JAUGEN
I have already told you the length of it.

                    BEN
True, but I must go and see Sting to here it
firsthand.

INT. STING'S HOUSE - DAY

Ben walks up to Sting's house and nods to the Guard outside.

                    BEN
I am here to see Sting.

                    STING'S GUARD
Go right in. He is in the meeting hall.

Ben goes inside where Sting and other MEMBERS from the village are addressing
Narmer's visit.

                    BEN
My good men. Good morning to you all.

                    STING
Ben, welcome my friend. It is good to see
that you have not cower away like a
frighten dog, in these times of
uncertainty.

                    BEN
That is not my way of doing things. I have
come to see how I could be of any
assistance. After all, I do feel somewhat
responsible for what is going on.

                    STING
You are in no way responsible for any of
this confusion that is going on.
          (to everyone)

None of you for that matter. The landings
would have gone on with or without you.
You simply paid for a service that could
be provided, and it was.

                    BEN
So with this new proclamation from the
Empire, what is our next course of action?

                    STING
As of right now we haven't any options.
So as of now we are just going to sit back,
and let the Kushites be Kushites. Time
will pass, and as usual they will have
forgiven us, or forgotten about the
landings, and will have moved on to other
affairs.

                    BEN
Is that good enough, for us to feel secure in?

                    STING
Good enough for me. Forgiveness and
amnesia has been two known consistent
characteristic traits of the Kushites since
first contact.

                    BEN
I really hope that to be true, because I see
nothing to be gained from a conflict with
the Empire.

                    MEMBER 1
There's always the booty from the spoils
of victory.

                    BEN
Yes, if we were to win. And from my
perspective that is a huge if.

EXT. BUBA VILLAGE - DAY

Beirut and his company ride through the village of Buba. They head toward Sting's
house.

EXT. BEN'S HOUSE - DAY

Lena and Srtife sit talking when Jaugen passes them headed through the gate.

                    SRTIFE
          Hey Jaugen.

Srtife walks over to Jaugen.

                    SRTIFE
          Where are you going?

                    JAUGEN
          I'm stepping out for a moment. Why?

                    SRTIFE
          Why? Didn't Ben just leave here telling us
          all to stay here?

                    JAUGEN
          Us all, being you and your father. Doing
          my shear of the labor is the only orders I
          am obligated to take from Ben.

Jaugen walks by them and through the gate headed to town.

EXT. BUBA - DAY

Jaugen gets to the town streets, and starts heading toward the town center. Beirut
and his company approach him from behind.

He turns to see what's coming when him and Beirut make eye contact. Jaugen tries
to turn away, but Beirut recognizes him.

                    BEIRUT
          Woo, woo.

He stops his horse.

                    BEIRUT
          Fast Jaugen is that you? I thought that
          looked like you. It has been a couple of
          seasons since the last time I seen you.

JAUGEN
(hesitates)
Ah. Ye-ye yah. Yah, yes it has. How have
life been treating you.

BEIRUT
I always knew your words meant nothing.
But, I could not have guessed that you
owing me five pounds of gold would have
led to me never seeing you again.

JAUGEN
Oh, that. I haven't forgotten about it, I just
haven't been to Sais in a while.

BEIRUT
Sure, if you say so. Look never mind that,
that is all in the pass.

JAUGEN
(surprised)
Are you sure? I do intend to repay you.

BEIRUT
Certainly, the Delta as a community has a
much bigger issues on which we must
stand together and address. To let
something so insignificant, have us
avoiding each other.

JAUGEN
I definitely agree.

BEIRUT
You should, I know you miss your former
life at the gold mines in the south.

JAUGEN
The best days of my life.

BEIRUT
Are you ready and willing to seize the
opportunity, to live a hundred folds better
than that.

                         JAUGEN
          I'm listening.

                         BEIRUT
          I am headed to the square now to see
          Sting. Keep an ear out, for a campaign
          towards a better tomorrow.

Beirut rides off as Jaugen watches.

EXT. STING'S HOUSE - DAY

Beirut addresses the Guard, who send him inside to see Sting.

INT. STING'S HOUSE - DAY

                         MEMBER 2
          It's not as if we would not stand a chance
          at all.

                         BEN
          This is not a matter of standing a chance.
          With life there is always a chance. But the
          fact still remains, the odds are against us.
          So if a conflict could be avoided, I suggest
          we do so.

                         MEMBER 1
          Conflicts are a part of life. I see no reason
          to run away from them.

Beirut enters the room. Everyone gets quiets. He walks past the village members
and right up to Sting.

                         BEIRUT
          Sting my friend and comrade. Good day to
          you my friend.
                    (to Village Members)
          And the same to your guests. A good day to
          you all.

                         VILLAGE MEMBERS
          Good morning.

STING

And a good morning to you also my friend.
Welcome once again to Buba.

BEIRUT

Thank you, it is always a pleasure to come
here. Your community has remarkable
hospitality.

STING

You are too gracious. To what, do I owe the
pleasure of your visit?

BEIRUT

Oh, Just a word in private.

STING

Would you gentlemen pardon me, until
further notice?

The Village Members leave.

BEIRUT
(to Sting)
There should be no questions as to why I
am here. At this present time my
problems are yours and the rest of the
Delta's.

STING

I am aware of that. But I have no way to
oppose it, so I have accepted it.

BEIRUT

You have accepted it? It sounds as if you
are getting weak on me. A lot could be
done with your community coming
together with the rest of the Delta, and
playing your part.

STING

Playing our part. What on Earth are you
talking about?

BEIRUT

It is certainly not rolling over, and playing dead for these Kushites. No, I 'm talking about standing together and reaching for the prize, reaching for the wealth, and the power that the Nile Valley has to offer.
(beat)
And other than the fertile soil we farm on, the wealth of the Nile is inland southwards.

STING

I 'm listening.

BEIRUT

Don't you think it is full time now that you and your people get control of some of that wealth?
(beat)
Sais feels so, and we are ready to reach for our portion.

STING

Sais feels so. Oh great, now all we need to do is band together, and over throw the Empire.
(beat)
Look, there is nothing I would rather do than to drive my spear through the hearts of the lot of those Kushites, especially that of Narmer. But even with the entire Delta united that will still be a mountain too steep to climb.

BEIRUT

But how could we not attempt that climb. When at the top of that mountain awaits our glory? Even a failed attempt would be worth the try.

STING

Oh let us be clear, it is not the climb that concerns me. But the sure fall to death.

To live your life and not reach for glory,
only means that your potential has
already fallen to its death.
        (beat)
You were born here in the Nile Valley.
True this is the Kushites native land, left
to them by their ancestors, but you
descent from them and have every right
to your shear of this land. Still they do not
honor your birthright. They classify you
all as a Foreigners, marginalizing the
majority of the Mulattos with us up here
in the Delta. Limiting you all just as they
have limited us. Meanwhile the Kushites
strongholds are the inlands containing
mines of gold, silver, diamonds, ivory,
iron, and all sorts of other riches that they
keep to themselves. I don't know about
you, but I for one have grown frustrated
of these limits and restrictions. And I am
now ready to climb that mountain and
take my glory.

                STING
The prize does sound very tempting but let
us be realistic. How could a population of
approximately fifty thousand, half of which
are women and children, overthrow the
Kushite Empire?

                BEIRUT
This that I am about to tell you, is the
assurance that I promise to all my Delta
comrades in our pursuit of liberty.
        (beat)
What if I was to tell you we have twenty
thousand trained fighters in the old
country ready to come and fight alongside
the Delta.

                STING
Well, now you are beginning to make
more sense. These fighters in your old
country, is there a guarantee that they
will come to your aid.

                         BEIRUT
              Guaranteed. They were assembled for this
              sole purpose. They have boats ready to
              sail as soon as they get the word.

                         STING
              I see. Now you are beginning to paint a
              better portrait.
                    (beat)
              I tell you what, if you guarantee me with
              victory I will get more trade routes, a
              portion of the mines captured, and more
              land for my people. I promise you, upon
              arrival of your fighters, the Buba
              community will faithfully join your
              campaign.

                         BEIRUT
              With the Kushite Empire no longer in
              power. That leaves the trade routes,
              numerous mines, and land to the
              conquerors to do with what we will.

Looks at each other serious. Beirut and Sting shake hands in agreement.
Beirut leaves.

                         BEIRUT
              Goodbye.

EXT. STING'S HOUSE - CONTINUOUS

The locals look on as Beirut mounts his horse and leaves. Sting comes out onto his
balcony and addresses his people. Jaugen pays attention from the CROWD.

                         STING
              The Delta have agreed to!

The crowd erupts with mixed feelings.

Beirut hears them CHEERING from the distance and smiles. Jaugen heads home.

INT. BEN'S HOUSE - DAY

Jaugen walks in full of excitement for the opportunity.

                    JAUGEN
        Sting has just agreed to support Beirut if
        there is a war against the Empire.

Everyone is surprised and stops what they're doing. Ben is confused.

EXT. ATHRA - DAY

Beirut and his company ride to Athra. The locals watch them when they arrive.
Beirut head straight through town to Donoe's house.

EXT. DONOE'S HOUSE - DAY

Beirut addresses the guard outside Donoe's house. The GUARD allows Beirut to go
inside.

INT. DONOE'S HOUSE - DAY

                    D MEMBER 1
        Am I to just sit aside, and let them take
        the little I've got?

                    DONOE
        The Kushites are not interested in taking
        the little you've got. They only want to
        make sure they still have control over
        their land. As long as they do not get any
        reason to take what you've got, they
        won't.

Donoe sees Beirut coming and clears the room.

                    DONOE
        Would you gentlemen pardon me for a
        moment.

The Athra Village members get up and leave.

                    BEIRUT
        I see you still have your peacemaker
        persona going strong.

                    DONOE
        I figured it has gotten me this far, why
        abandon it.

They shake hands.

> BEIRUT
>
> Donoe, my comrade it has been a long time.

> DONOE
>
> Too long, but as usual it is always good to see you my friend.

Beirut gets some refreshments and makes himself comfortable.

> BEIRUT
>
> So, how do the people of Athra feel about this new proclamation from the Kushites.

> DONOE
>
> They will depict this situation as whatever I portray it to be. I hope this visit from you means that you and Kalili are ready to utilize our fighters back in the old country.

> BEIRUT
>
> Why, do you feel it is time?

> DONOE
>
> I 'm not sure, but this is the best chance I have seen yet. And time is not on my side. I am getting older by the seasons, and I have only got one or two healthy ones left. And there is nothing I would rather do before my time ends, than to give my all in a battle. To feel the thrill, which only come from fighting for one's own life.

Beirut lifts his mug.

> BEIRUT
>
> My friend it is good to see that you are as eager as ever. For yes, I have come here to let you know that our time to strike has come.

EXT. KING SALO'S PALACE - DAY

Chief Narmer arrives at the King's palace. He gives his horse to a handler and addresses the Guard who allows him inside.

INT. KING SALO'S PALACE - DAY

Chief Narmer walks into the study to find the King sitting.

                    KING SALO
          Chief Narmer welcome.

                    CHIEF NARMER
               (kneels)
          Greetings my King.

                    KING SALO
          Please, make your-self comfortable.

Narmer sits down.

                    CHIEF NARMER
          Thank you.

                    KING SALO
          So, how was your visit to the Delta, how
          were you received by the residents?

                    CHIEF NARMER
          From their reaction, it is a must that we
          put a stop to the Foreigners operating
          freely in the Delta. They have developed
          the mentality that they belong here, and
          the Empire cannot tell them otherwise.
          Only Donoe and Kwame seemed genuine,
          when saying they knew nothing of the
          landings. Beirut and Kalili as expected
          were very arrogant with their reaction. As
          if they feel they could tell me anything and
          I must accept it. Three of their residents
          actually charged me, declaring they will
          fight to the death for the Delta.

KING SALO
(surprised)
Three men charged you. Are you serious?
(beat)
How did you handle it?

CHIEF NARMER
I gave them what they were looking for.
Death delivered as swift as their words.

KING SALO
(beat)
And what about the other villages, what
were their reactions?

CHIEF NARMER
Sting and the Mulatto population are truly
going to be a problem. Them along with
Sais, were the ones in particular who
seems to think that they do not have to
answer to the Empire. As we left Buba,
there was a roar of resentment so loud
behind us. It was heard as far as the Nile.
As for the city of Rumah, they were
worried and disappointed about our
decision, but no obvious resentment was
shown.

KING SALO
Giving them a proclamation was
absolutely the right thing to do.
(beat)
If the new comers of the Delta things that
they have come along far enough, that
they feel they could react this hostile
towards the Empire. Then it is time we
tame the beast, before it grows too wild
and become uncontrollable.
(beat)
Have you notified the other tribes.

CHIEF NARMER
Yes, I have sent messages to inform them
all.

                    KING SALO
List anything, and everything you will need
to be prepared in case there is a war.

                    CHIEF NARMER
We won't need much, just a fleet of boats,
encase we need a swift attack up the Nile.
Enough to carry at least five entire units of
warriors and there Calvary of horses, plus
a second fleet of boats for reinforcement,
and enough arrows and spears so that no
warrior would not be over equipped. Just
to make sure that we put an end to these
foreign parasites once and for all.

INT. DONOE'S HOUSE - DAY

                    DONOE
Yes I 'm sure, it was turned back over to
Jusa after a meeting held in Nekheb by the
council.

                    BEIRUT
So if I was to visit the Mumon village right
now, I would find Jusa there back in
control.

                    DONOE
Yes, the Mumons are no longer in
captivity. I am not sure of the condition of
the people, or their village, but they are
back in control.

                    BEIRUT
That is excellent, that gives us back our
inside on the Empire's Chiefs and
warriors.

                    DONOE
Are you sure informing Jusa will be a wise
idea? I mean the issue is war, and the
sides will basically be determined by
cultures. Are you sure you could depend
on the Mumons to turn their back on their
people, and side with us.

                    BEIRUT
          Jusa is a greedy, coldhearted savage, who
          will do anything for wealth and power. I
          know exactly how to negotiate with Jusa,
          you don't have to worry about him. Just
          see about getting your people ready.

                    DONOE
          Consider it done. The people of Athra will
          be ready as soon as the words roll off of
          my tongue.

                    BEIRUT
          Then my friend I say to you, prepare
          yourself to have the time of your life.

He stands to say farewell.

                    BEIRUT
          I will send word to keep you informed on
          our strategy.

                    DONOE
          You do so.

They shake hands.

                    BEIRUT
          Until that time, you just be prepared to
          find your thrills.

                    DONOE
          I look forward to the hunt. Just you be
          sure to stay safe on your journey.

Beirut nods and leaves.

EXT. DONOE'S HOUSE - DAY

Beirut mounts his horse and rides off with his company.

EXT. VILLAGES - DAY/NIGHT MONTAGE

Beirut and his company ride for a while. The sun begins to set. The day turns to
night.

EXT. VILLAGES - DAY

Beirut and his company rise with the sun. They head toward the next village. The group rides for a while.

EXT. MUMON VILLAGE - DAY

Beirut and his company arrive at the Mumon village. They notice that the structures are still damaged. Smoke is still coming from some of them.

The air is still foggy and PEOPLE are still in distress. The Mumon WOMEN and CHILDREN are cooking and helping to clear debris, while the MUMON MEN are working nonstop reconstructing the village.

Jusa sits on his balcony that overlooks the town. He sees the posse coming through the village, so do the locals. Beirut, and company goes to Jusa's house.

> BEIRUT
> Congratulations to you old friend. I heard
> the Mumon village was turned back over
> to you, so I had to come and congratulate
> you in person.

> JUSA
> I'm positive you did not leave your
> comfortable home in Sais, to come here
> and congratulate me.

> BEIRUT
> Then why are we still talking outside?

Jusa signals to his guard to let them in.

INT. JUSA HOUSE - DAY

> JUSA
> I attended the meeting held by the
> council, so there is no reason to act as if
> all is well in the Delta.

> BEIRUT
> Was it necessary for such a harsh, unfair
> decision from your brothers, towards the
> people of the Delta?

JUSA

Hah, my brothers. Did you not notice the damage to my village, resulting from the Aswan's attack? Not to mention the countless lives lost, plus the gold and land I had to give to the Aswan people.
(beat)
A judgment my so call brothers thinks is equivalent to the life of three worthless women.

BEIRUT

It seems as if the people of the Delta are not the only ones, affected by the Empire's brand of justice.

JUSA

True the Mumons have our own issues to sort out, but anything directly frowned upon by Chief Narmer, is a problem within a problem.

BEIRUT

Chief Narmer has never showed me a friendly face, so his frowns I have gotten quite use to. But you...
(beat)
What about you, where do you stand on this issue?

JUSA

I will tell you just as I have told the Council. The Mumon people have our own problems to deal with, and don't have the strength to take a stand on no issue.
(beat)
Why, why do you wish to know where I stand?

BEIRUT

You have been a good friend, someone with whom the Delta has always had a positive relationship. I 'm just curious to know how you viewed the new comers of the Delta.

JUSA

I have no problem, with the Foreigners of the Delta.

BEIRUT

Likewise, the people of the Delta have no problem with the Empire. But ever since the visit from Chief Narmer the Foreign population of the Delta have been in an up roar. They are all paranoid and uncertain of what the Empire may do.

JUSA

At the meeting the perception I got from the Council, was one of, if the Delta were to stop the landings, you all will be left alone.

BEIRUT

There is no telling who or when that request will be violated. These times are different from that of old, when Sais was the only foreign influence in the Delta. Now many other villages have sprung up with leaders and minds of their own. There is just no sure way to prevent the landings from happening again.

JUSA

It sounds as if the Delta is faced with a real dilemma.

BEIRUT

Yes we are, and there are already talk going around of the new comers vowing to fight to the death.

JUSA

Well I hope that you have at least assured them, that if they raise arms against the Empire. Fighting to their deaths is exactly what they will be doing.

                    BEIRUT
If put in a situation where they are about
to lose everything. What do they have to
lose if they put up a fight for it first?

                    JUSA
          (nods)
The way you speak it is obvious. You and
the Delta have already made up your
minds to fight.

                    BEIRUT
I wouldn't say have already made up our
minds. But instead, we are preparing for
the worst.

                    JUSA
Preparing for the worst, are you. If I may
ask how do you foreigners prepare for
death?

Jusa plays along.

                    JUSA
And also, why are you telling me all of
this?

                    BEIRUT
Because I would like to know if there was
a war, could I still consider you a friend?

                    JUSA
And what exactly would constitute me
being a friend, in a time of war.
Considering me being a member of the
Council of the Empire.

                    BEIRUT
You and the Mumon warriors not taking
part in a war against the Delta.

                    JUSA
You don't have to worry about us taking
part in any war, at least not until there is
some kind of spoil to be shared.
          (beat)

BEIRUT

What if I was to offer you one thousand
pounds of gold, to not join in at all?

JUSA

Now, there is the Beirut I know and
admire. This is the Beirut I have been
waiting on to appear. If you are willing to
offer us one thousand pounds of gold for
the Mumon warriors to not get involved,
what are you willing to offer for our
assistance if there is a war?

BEIRUT

If you were to somehow assist us in any
future war, I wouldn't have to make you
an offer. With the proper outcome, you
could easily end up one of the strongest
Chiefs and village, having the entire
Empire to govern. Even if your assistance
is not by way of fighting!

JUSA
(sarcastically)
With the proper outcome, I could have the
Empire to govern. Exactly what Empire
are we referring to, the Kushite Empire.
(laughs)
Haha, I hope I do not discourage you, but
what chance on Earth do the Delta have
against the mighty Kushite Empire.

BEIRUT

Don't you worry about that, let that be the
Delta's problem.

JUSA

That will be the Delta's mistake. But as
you have said, I will leave that up to you
and the Delta to sort out. As for me, any
involvement from me, I shall be
compensated in advance.

                    BEIRUT
It sounds simple enough. How involved
are you willing to get?

                    JUSA
For the right fee!

Jusa sits back with a sinister grin on his face.

INT. BEN'S HOUSE - DAY

                    ALSI
I do not care if the Delta would be making
a terrible mistake. If there is a war against
the Kushites, I will be standing with the
people of the Delta.

                    BEN
I 'm not questioning whom you should
stand with. But these are not the people
one rush to war against. What chance
does the Delta have against the Kushites?
They easily out number us twenty to one.
And that is just counting there warriors,
to every man, woman, and child of the
Delta.

                    ALSI
Beirut and the people of Sais must think
the Delta have a chance, why else would
he be going around, encouraging the
people of the Delta to take a stand
together.

                    BEN
Yes, he does think he have a chance, a
chance to manipulate the people of the
Delta into fighting a war that could get
him more wealth and power. Look you do
not know this man. He is not to be
trusted.

JAUGEN
(sarcastically)
A chance for wealth and power, I will
probably give up the odds on that in any
situation.

SRTIFE
(laughs)
As will I.

BEN
I haven't the slightest clue as to why you
all are in such a haste to give your lives
away.

ALSI
Cousin I know you are familiar with the
characters of this country, and true in
deed Beirut is probably not to be trusted.
But the only thing my life is in a rush for,
are better days. And if the only way I see
to make those better days manifest is
through battle, then it will be swords
drawn, in a forward march. And to
anything that stands in my path, that
sword I will drive through their heart.

BEN
Well it's obvious it makes no sense talking
to the three of you. You all have already
made up your minds on what you intend
to do.

ALSI
Cousin I do not want you to feel as if I do
not see your point of view, or do not
respect it. It is just that I came to the Nile
Valley, with dreams of getting a piece of
the wealth that is rumored to be here. I
also know you have been here a while and
this was not the way you came about your
wealth, or even the way you would advise
someone else to go about getting theirs.
But I have just arrived fresh from the old
country with nothing to lose, and I aim to

seize every opportunity I can to get my
share of that wealth.

                    BEN
Then it is like I have said, It makes no
sense talking to you about this issue. Your
mind is already made up on what you
intend to do.

Ben stands, disappointed.

                    BEN
I will be in the town, I need to know the
price that was worth the life of every man,
woman, and child of the Buba.

Ben walks off, leaving them standing there.

                    JAUGEN
Never mind him, there is only one way to
earn something in life and that is by
working for it. No matter what that work
may be. Truth be told, if there is a war,
none of us would be able to escape it even
if we wanted to. If there is a war, Ben will
be on the front line like the rest of us,
fighting for the Delta.

INT. JUSA HOUSE - DAY

                    JUSA
Then when I see the right opportunity, I
will send two units of marks-men into
different sections of the battlefield, to pick
off key members of the Empire's warriors,
which will disrupt their chain of
command.

                    BEIRUT
Are you sure, you will have the manpower
to carry out such an operation.

                    JUSA
Never you mind our current state, or
manpower. You just have my payment of

five hundred thousand pounds of gold delivered and it will be done.

                    BEIRUT
Very well then, if it ever comes to that, I will have it delivered to you at the first sign of trouble.

Beirut stands to leave.

                    BEIRUT
I thank you once again for your continual friendship Chief Jusa, the entire Delta thanks you.

                    JUSA
I do not want your thanks. We both simply made an agreement with intentions on profiting something.

                    BEIRUT
Which is a good enough reason for me. I look forward to, and will greatly appreciate your assistance, if that time ever comes.

                    JUSA
You have my word, upon delivery of my fee. The Mumon warriors and myself will faithfully support you and the Delta in your endeavors.

They shake hands.

                    BEIRUT
I must be on my way. Until such time old friend!

                    JUSA
Until such time.

Beirut exits.

INT. BUBA MEETING HALL - DAY

Ben disappointed, visits Sting. He Walks inside the Buba meeting hall and sees the Village Members all having a good time. He looks around, and walks over to Sting.

                    BEN
              (to Sting)
    What is the meaning of all this?

                    STING
    What is the meaning of what?

                    BEN
    Why would your intentions suddenly
    change from waiting out the Kushites, to
    now taking part in any future war?

                    STING
    Ben, you are a good man, know yourself
    and take heed of the way you speak to me.

                    BEN
    I mean no disrespect, but why would you
    choose to put the people of Buba in harm
    way.

                    STING
    I do not want a war against the Kushites,
    but with the future looking like a war is
    inevitable, regardless of if it is our fault or
    not. I must prepare our people for the
    worst, while working towards our best
    interest.

                    BEN
    And our best interest is, in taking sides
    with Beirut?

                    STING
    And who are we suppose to take sides
    with, the Kushites. I don't know how you
    perceive things here in the Nile Valley, but
    the bottom line is. It is us against them,
    the north against the south, the
    Foreigners against the natives, the Delta
    against Kemet.

> BEN
> I understand there is only the Delta to
> stand with in the time of war, but why
> would you allow either Beirut or Kalili to
> be the ones to lead us into that war. I mean
> those two do nothing without an ulterior
> motive, why are they going about rallying
> the residents of the Delta to fight. They
> could just as easy, be going about telling
> everyone to see to it there are no more
> landings. What are they looking to gain?

> STING
> I do not know what they are looking to
> gain, but I do know if there is a war and
> the Delta lose, we all lose.

EXT. KURU VILLAGE - DAY

Beirut and company ride into Kuru village. They get to the town streets and head to
Zomi's residence. The locals look on. Beirut addresses Zomi's Guard from his horse.

> BEIRUT
> Good day. I was hoping to have a word
> with Chief Zomi.

> Z GUARD
> I'm surprised to see you here considering
> everything that is going on.

> BEIRUT
> There should be no surprise in me visiting
> an old friend. Is the Chief available for
> visitors?

> Z GUARD
> Wait here a moment.

The guard goes inside for a while, then returns.

> Z GUARD
> Come with me.

Beirut gets off his horse and follows the guard inside.

INT. ZOMI'S HOUSE - DAY

Zomi waits for Beirut. Beirut enters with the guard.

                    BEIRUT
          (bows)
     Good day to you Chief Zomi. Thank you
     for seeing me.

                    ZOMI
          (nods)
     Welcome. We are old associates. The least
     I could do is see you, after you have
     traveled from so far. So exactly what have
     brought you to Kuru?

                    BEIRUT
     I'm just passing through the south to visit
     some of my old associates such as your-
     self, to see if the entire Empire feels the
     same way about the Delta, as Chief
     Narmer does.

                    ZOMI
     I'm not sure, how does Chief Narmer feel
     about the Delta.

                    BEIRUT
     Well as of recent we certainly do not seem
     to be on his list of favorite people.

                    ZOMI
     Neither Chief Narmer, nor the Empire
     dislike the people of the Delta. The
     Empire has a problem with the
     continuous landings of more and more
     foreigners.

                    BEIRUT
     I understand the frustration of the
     Empire, but there are countless people in
     the Delta who have nothing to do with the
     landings. Why should everyone be
     punished along with the wrong doers?

ZOMI

If the Delta cares so much about their
innocent residents, then I suggest you all
come together, and put an end to the
landings. Because I for one stand with and
support the Empire in our decision!

BEIRUT

Despite our years of friendship, you
would support the Empire in raging war
against the Delta?

ZOMI

Yes, over the years we have developed a
prosperous trade relationship. But
stopping the landings will secure the
future of my Nation.

BEIRUT

I too support the securing of one's nation
future. That is what I wish to do in the
Delta. A large population of my old
country men have migrated there. But
should security come at the expense of so
many innocent people.

ZOMI

If there come to be any innocent victims
in the Delta. It will be the fault of the
residents of the Delta. You all could not
have asked for a better second chance. All
the Empire asks is that the Delta live up to
their agreement of the treaty.

BEIRUT

The Foreigners, who have been here long
enough to know, honor the treaty. It is the
new comers who-

ZOMI

There is really no reason to speak any
further on the issue. Bottom line is, either
the landings stops, or the Empire will take
back full control of the Delta, which I am
in full support of.
        (beat)

Is there anything else you wish to address?

> BEIRUT
> No, the proclamation is the length of it.

> ZOMI
> Well my friend, my advice to you is to encourage the Delta to be wise. Their future is in their hands.

> BEIRUT
> I thank you for your time and your advice Chief Zomi.

Beirut stands to leave.

> ZOMI
> I just hope that you take it for what it's worth.

> BEIRUT
> I will, once again thank you old friend.

Beirut bows in respect. Zomi nods in respect.

> BEIRUT
> I must be on my way. I hope the next time we see each other peace is still the order of the day.

> ZOMI
> Let us hope so. Until next time, have a safe journey.

Beirut leaves.

EXT. ZOMI'S HOUSE - DAY

Beirut mounts his horse and heads toward the next village. The locals watch as they leave.

EXT. VILLAGES - DAY

Beirut and his company ride to the next village.

EXT. KERMA VILLAGE - DAY

Beirut and his company arrive at Kerma. They head toward the local leader's house. The locals gaze at them as they ride through the town. Beirut and his company stop outside Popa's house.

EXT. POPA'S HOUSE - DAY

Beirut addresses the guard. The Guard lets them inside.

INT. POPA'S HOUSE - DAY

Beirut and Popa greets each other.

INT. POPA'S HOUSE - LATER

In the middle of their conversation.

> POPA
> I was one of the few members of the council who felt that the proclamation was too sudden and too harsh. So I can assure you. Myself, nor my village will not take part in a campaign just because of the landings. But I cannot say the same for the rest of the Empire, so my advice to you is to convince the residents of the Delta to stop the practice.

> BEIRUT
> I am trying my best. I thank you once again for having understanding in this matter, so far only you have shown any sympathy for the innocent people of the Delta. Your heart is truly weightless. The Ntchru will reward you. You are a true reflection of their attributes.

> POPA
> To see justice and honor amongst men would be reward enough for me.

Beiruit stands with a sinister smile.

                         BEIRUT
            Only if both sides could halt for a moment
            and take a lesson from you, perhaps we
            would be able to resolve all of this
            confusion.

                         POPA
            Perhaps, but you and I both know that
            will never happen.

                         BEIRUT
            Unfortunately, no it will not. But as long
            as there are understandings like yours
            and mines, there is always hope.

                         POPA
            Yes there is.

                         BEIRUT
            Let us hope good fortune continue to
            permit us more meetings like this in the
            future.

Beirut bows to Popa in respect. Popa nods in respect.

                         BEIRUT
            Until next time old friend.

                         POPA
            Let us hope so, until next time.

Beirut exits.

EXT. POPA'S HOUSE - DAY

Beirut mounts his horse and rides off with his company. The Locals looks on
curiously at them as they pass through.

EXT. KURGUS VILLAGE - DAY

Beirut and his company reach Kurgus. The locals pay attention as they ride through
the town going to visit Duka the local leader.

EXT. DUKA'S HOUSE - DAY

They arrive outside Duka's house and address the Guard who takes them inside.

INT. DUKA'S HOUSE - DAY

Duka is in the middle of a meeting when they walk in. Beirut bows to greet Duka. Duka is surprised to see Beirut.

                    DUKA
          Beirut, welcome.
                    (to the Village Members)
          Please leave us in private.

They sit.

                    BEIRUT
          Thank you for seeing me. I have a very
          serious problem from Chief Narmer and
          the rest of the Council.

                    DUKA
          Yes, I know. I was there at the meeting
          when the council made their decision.
          This is a very unfortunate situation that
          the Delta has found them-selves in.

                    BEIRUT
          I am well aware of that fact. I am from the
          Delta. Sais town hall have not closed since
          the proclamation, our residents are
          terrified trying to figure out what to do.

                    DUKA
          I sympathize with you all, because I
          glimpse a portion of their uncertainty
          through the foreign population here in
          Kurgus. Even though the threat is
          hundreds of miles away, the Foreigners
          here are still paranoid, fearing what
          tomorrow may bring.

                    BEIRUT
          I am fortunate that you are able to see our
          uncertainty for yourself. What would you
          suggest the Delta do under these
          circumstances?

DUKA

I would advise you all to see to it that the landings stop. Or prepare to defend yourselves. Whichever of the two you all think is in the best interest off the foreign population of the Delta, because I assure you it will be one of the two.

BEIRUT

From where I stand in the Delta, those are two battles that I cannot win.

Beirut tries to get sympathy.

BEIRUT

Can't you talk to the other members of the Council, and try to convince them to handle this situation some other way.

DUKA

Trust me I have tried. But evidently Chief Narmer, who is spear heading this campaign, is convinced that this is the only negotiation that the foreign population of the Delta will respect.

BEIRUT

And what about you, do you support Chief Narmer and his method of negotiation?

DUKA

We have done a lot of trading together, I consider you a financial asset. Not a threat.

BEIRUT

I thank you for being a loyal friend.
            (beat)
But, there are so many innocent people in the Delta, isn't there anything we could do to convince your brothers to reconsider.

DUKA

Chief Narmer mind has already been made up. The only ones capable of helping the Delta, is the Delta. Your faiths

will be determined by how you all choose
to deal with this matter.
(beat)
The only help I could offer is perhaps a
safe refuge in my village, for all those who
are innocent and wishes not to be
involved in any future confusion.

                    BEIRUT
This is a very gracious offer from you
Chief Duka. The Delta will praise you for
such an offer.
(sarcastically)
But could your village take the entire
Delta, because the moment they hear of
this every man, woman, and child will be
trying to migrate here to your village.

                    DUKA
That wouldn't be a problem at all. There
is more than enough unused land on the
outskirts of my village. The innocent
population of the Delta is more than
welcome to it. Just be sure to advise them
to travel as nomads, and arrive with their
own food and shelter.

                    BEIRUT
You are actually serious.

                    DUKA
Why wouldn't I be? I know there are
countless innocent Foreigners in the Delta
whom have no part in, and want no part
in what's going on. By allowing them to
come here, the Empire wouldn't
persecute them with the violators of the
Delta if there were any future violation of
the treaty.

Beirut stands.

                    BEIRUT
Chief Duka. I thank you for your more than
gracious offer. The entire Delta thanks you.

                              DUKA
          If you or the Delta would like to thank me,
          show it through your action. For your
          own benefit, see to it that the landings
          stop, to avoid any future conflicts.

                             BEIRUT
          I give you my word. I will do everything in
          my power, to see to it that the landings
          stops.

                              DUKA
          I 'm sure it will be in the Delta's best
          interest to do so.

Duka nods.

                             BEIRUT
                              (bow)
          I thank you for your kindness. You are a
          true friend and a good man. It is an honor
          for me to call you my friend.

                              DUKA
          You 're welcome. Have a safe journey.

                             BEIRUT
          I will, thank you friend.

Beirut nods and leaves.

EXT. DUKA'S HOUSE - NIGHT

Beirut exits the house, mounts his horse, and leaves with his company. Locals
continue to look on as they pass. Beirut and company gladly head for home.

EXT. VILLAGES - NIGHT

MONTAGE:

-Beirut and his company ride headed home. The sun rises. The sun sets. The moon
rises. The moon sets. The sun rises. The sun sets. The moon rises.

EXT. SAIS - NIGHT

Beirut and his company return to Sais. Locals look on. Beirut rides to his compound, hands his horse to a handler, and goes inside to update Kalili.

INT. KALILI HOUSE - NIGHT

Beirut walks in a gets a drink of water.

> BEIRUT
> So what is the status in the Delta?

Kalili is lounging in a sea of WOMEN.

> KALILI
> All is well. I spoke to Rah and Kwame in
> the north, and they both agreed to give
> their support. Also our message arrived in
> the old country two days ago.

Kalili lifts his mug.

> KALILI
> All is well.

Beirut sits back, relaxes.

> BEIRUT
> That is good.

> KALILI
> The message is with one of our most
> reliable courier. A reply should be here
> five days from today.

> BEIRUT
> That is good. Real good.

> KALILI
> And how about you, how was your visit to
> the south.

> BEIRUT
> It could not have gone better. Chief Duka
> even made us a very advantageous offer.

Beirut sits back with a sinister grin.

EXT. NEKHEB VILLAGE - DAY

Chief Narmer is riding in a carriage. He is dressed in all white. As he passes through the town, him and the residents observe each other. They stop what they 're doing to hail Narmer.

The prosperity and lifestyle of the Nekheb community is on full display. CHILDREN run happily, playing with each other as they pass a barbershop.

At the barbershop MEN of all ages socialize, and wait for a haircut.

A stall over, a MAN and WOMAN are getting body paint.

A WOMAN walks by with her BABY tied to her. She goes to a stall two stalls down. She stops there to look at animal skins and different types materials stitched as clothes.

A MAN calls out.

                    MAN
          Sandals. Sandals for sale! Sandals, I have
          the latest in all-purpose footwear! Sandals
          for sale guaranteed to shield your feet
          from the roughest of surfaces!

A LADY passes by, being escorted by her SERVANT. The man tries to sell her sandals.

                    MAN
          My fair lady, would you like to buy a pair
          of new footwear for your servant? It is
          guaranteed to able him to do twice the
          labor.

                    LADY
          I 'm not interested.

She goes into the stall next to it and look at spices. Across the street a WOMAN sits in front of her stall weaving baskets when a MAN with a DONKEY comes up to her to buy a new hamper.

She stands and shows the man different types of hampers. He tries them on the Donkey.

OTHER PEOPLE walk past, going about their daily lives.

The stall next to the basket weaver is a wood carver. Next to that is a pottery maker. Next to that is a portrait painter who is painting a portrait of a WOMAN and her DAUGHTER.

A few stalls down is a WOMAN selling different fruits, vegetables, and yams. The stall next to her is selling meat. Next to that is a wine bar.

It's a fully-functioning community. The residents continue to hail Narmer as he pass.

Chief Narmer's carriage arrives at a beautiful temple. The outside is made from red stone bricks, coasted with gold dust to reflect light.

EXT. TEMPLE - DAY

The temple is finely decorated with writing, portraits on the walls. Statues of the Ntchru and their ancestors are lining the perimeter.

The Ntchru statues are carved with their specific attributes, representing the different aspects of the Creator of the Universe and her chosen light Atun Ra.

EXT. TEMPLE - DAY

Chief Narmer arrives at the temple. One of his SERVANTS opens the carriage door. TWO MEN stands guard at the entrance of the temple.

Narmer walks up and nods to the Guards as he passes.

Narmer walks up to TWO MORE GUARDS, both with a spear one across the other blocking the door. Narmer gets to the second entrance and they let him through.

INT. TEMPLE - DAY

Chief Narmer walks through a colorful hallway. The light gets darker the further he goes in.

INT. ROOM - DAY

Narmer gets to the end of the long hallway and there is a giant statue. He kneels down. He prays.

                    CHIEF NARMER
          Thank you Almighty Ntchru for
          continuing to be my everything. Thank
          you all for being my light, allowing me to

see through all situations. Thank you all
for being my strength, and removing all
fears from my heart. Thank you all for
continually providing for me, giving me
all the necessities I need in life. Thank you
all for continually protecting me through
every step of my life. This is why I sing
praises to you all Almighty Ntchru. You all
have resurrected me. You all have shined
your light of prosperity on me.

When Narmer finishes, he stands up and takes an unlit torch.

Narmer lights the flame and walks to one of the corners, which reveals a MAN in the
dark, in front of a passageway.

Narmer stands directly in front of him. The man waves a spiritual wand above and
alongside Narmer, blessing him. He lets Narmer pass.

INT. PASSAGEWAY

Narmer walks through the passageway. Narmer presses a couple of the bricks on
the wall, which opens a secret door in the floor.

Narmer enters, goes down a winding staircase, which leads Him to a meeting hall.
The meeting hall is decorated with cultural, and spiritual sacred artworks.

All the MEMBERS of the keepers of the order are assembled around a big conference
table having a meeting. Narmer walks over to a statue of Atun Ra, kneels and prays.

The members stand while Narmer prays.

                    CHIEF NARMER
          Praises be to you almighty father of our
          order of light. Thank you for removing the
          cover from our eyes, allowing us to see
          that which isn't in eyes sight.

Chief Narmer stands. All the memebrs put their hands over their hearts and says.

                    ALL MEMBERS
          All hail Atun Ra.

Narmer sits down and addresses the leader.

CHIEF NARMER
Pardon me brother for being late, I was
delayed by-

LEADER
There is no need to explain, for there is no
acceptable explanation. Your tardiness
will be overlooked on this one occasion,
but if you wish to continue to grow in this
brotherhood, your punctuality must be as
reliable as your loyalty.

CHIEF NARMER
(nods)
It will not happen again.

LEADER
I hope not.
        (to another Keeper)
Continue.

FIRST KEEPER
(stands)
Yes, thank you. As I was saying, the
sample in front of you is the extraction
from the newly tested coca leaf. When
extracted from the plant, it could be
applied to an open wound to minimize the
pain while the patient is being treated.
Test have also shown that when the leaf is
chewed, and it enters the blood stream it
makes the subject body numb, giving
healers the opportunity to set a broken
bone back into place. Giving the bone a
chance to heal itself properly. These
findings are remarkable. This new
medicine is much more favorable than
that of the puffer fish. For even though
they both make the body numb, the puffer
fish makes the subject weary, while the
coca leafs revives them.

LEADER
This is a very remarkable finding indeed.
Tell me have you seen any side effects?

FIRST KEEPER
No, none that we have seen as yet.

LEADER
And what about a wounded warrior on the battlefield, what affect will it have on them?

FIRST KEEPER
We have not tested the effects outside of injury recovery thus far, so I am not certain. But the effect should be a positive one, if taking into consideration the possible energy boost it might give a wounded warrior.

LEADER
When you do further testing, be sure to notify us.

FIRST KEEPER
I will be sure to do so.

He sits.

LEADER
And what of you second Keep, do you have any new discoveries or improvements you wish to shear with us.

SECOND KEEPER
No, not at this time.

LEADER
And how about you third Keep, are there any new developments you wish to shear with us.

THIRD KEEPER
Yes, there has been an improvement in our trade ventures. The other farmers and I have made an agreement with the goldsmiths in the hills of Meroe, to make Nekheb their chief provider of rice and yams. And I must say with Chief Narmer's son Djer remodeling our water pumps, to time and gage the distribution of water.

We will have no problems meeting our
Quota.

Third keep nods to Narmer in respect. Narmer was unaware, but nods back.

> LEADER
> Someone has remodeled the water pumps
> you say.

> THIRD KEEPER
> Yes, young Djer. It is quite innovating.

> LEADER
> Well you are the head of the order of
> farmers. If you are satisfied with the
> modification, it is good enough for me.

The Third Keeper nods, then sits.

> LEADER
> And how about you fourth Keeper, do you
> have anything you wish to shear with us.

> FOURTH KEEPER
> No, not at this moment.

> LEADER
> How about you fifth Keep, do you have
> any new developments you wish to shear
> with us?

> FIFTH KEEPER
> No, I have no new matter to address.

> LEADER
> And how about you sixth Keep, do you
> have anything you have anything new you
> wish to shear?

> SIXTH KEEPER
> Yes, I do have something I wish to shear
> with my fellow Keepers. The other brick
> masons and I have been mathematically
> measuring, and calculating trying to find a
> new approach to building levees. A new
> building concept that can combine with

our old designs and our successful
building materials that have already
worked for us.

                LEADER
A new construction concept, what exactly
have you been working on.

                SIXTH KEEPER
Ever since our ancestor started building
with earthen material such as stone in
Taseti, and Kemet. Our stone structures
and monuments have been indestructible
by man, and the natural Elements and
Forces of Mother Nun. Now with the
correct mathematical measurement, our
building concepts of erecting earthen
stone structures could be turned into a
project of levees, which could encompass
an entire village to keep the water out
during the yearly flood season.

                LEADER
What do you mean it will keep the water
out during the yearly flood season? Are
you intoxicated?

                SIXTH KEEPER
Yes, my lord. Intoxicated with inspiration.
Ever since the other stone masons and I
were summoned by Chief Narmer, whom
had the most brilliant, innovative idea of
how to divert the water of the Nile during
its yearly floods. This way the natives of
the low lands would not have to evacuate
during the flood season. Chief Narmer's
idea is to build from earthen material a
huge system of levees to control the water
level along the banks of the Nile,
stretching for approximately one
thousand kilometers.

                LEADER
I am not even going to carry on as if I fully
comprehend what you are expressing. But
you are the head of the order of stone

masonry, so I give you my blessing and look forward to seeing the finished product.

                    SIXTH KEEPER
Your wait will not be long. We 're in the middle of erecting a learning center for Chief Narmer and his teachers, once we are finish. The levees will be our next obligation.

                    LEADER
Keep us informed on the progress.

He nods, then turns to Chief Narmer and says.

                    LEADER
Speaking of learning, what are the updates for this quarter on the learning of the youths of Nekheb.

                    SEVENTH KEEPER
                    (stands)
All is well, the boys and girls of Nekheb are steadfast learning at a magnificent pace. The center being erected now, I intend to dedicate to all the elders of the village. I figured, the children under twelve have a compound where they go to learn. After age thirteen they are place in the field which they have excelled in to learn its history, and by age twenty they are placed in that field on active duty ending their learning in an institution. Unless being selected into the council of elders, which we all know is a slim chance. With a compound for the elders, ever man and woman from all fields, all trade, all industrial craftsman, all experts or apprentice, if they would like could come and have a place of total privacy to gather with their pears. A place where they could all exchange ideas, and still feels like a contributing member of a learning institution.

                    LEADER
I strongly support that idea. We have too
many worthy elders who are not being
honored. Keep me updated on your
progress as it manifest.
                    (beat)
How about you Eighth Keep, do you have
anything new to share with the order?

                    EIGHT KEEPER
                    (stands)
No my lord, not at this time. He sits.

                    LEADER
How about you Ninth Keep, do you have
anything new to share with us?

                    NINTH KEEPER
                    (stands)
Yes, I do. My diggers have found traces of
diamond in the hills of Jafet. We are
currently testing the minerals of the soil
before we dig any further.

                    LEADER
                    (surprised)
Diamond in Jafet. That would be a first,
but never the less it would be very
rewarding. You keep us updated on the
results.

He sits.

                    LEADER
How about you tenth keep, do you have
anything new to shear with us.

                    TENTH KEEPER
                    (stands)
No nothing new.

                    LEADER
How about you, eleventh Keep?

                    ELEVENTH KEEPER
          (stands)
All is well with the live stock, they are all
taking to their feed well, breeding
regularly, and are all looking very healthy.

                    LEADER
And how about you twelfth Keep, do you
have any new updates to share with us?

                    TWELFTH KEEPER
          (stands)
No, not at this time.

                    LEADER
Well then. That entails our progress
report for this season. Does anyone have
anything else they would like to add?

No replies.

                    LEADER
Okay then. Let us begin our annual
ceremony, honoring our savior, the greater
Light, the Light of all Lights, and father of
our order of light Atun Ra. For once again
being our light and prosperity through
another season. For shining your brilliant
light of enlightenment, that illuminates, and
gives life to the world.

Everyone stands and starts chanting. A door opens up behind them and a BABALU
PRIEST comes out with an animal. The Priest walks over to a sacrificial alter. The
Keepers follow. The Priest gets on the alter kills the animal, and then holds it up to
the sky as an offering.

The Keepers all reach in and take some of the blood. They all eat a piece of the raw
meat and smear the blood on their faces.

INT. BEN'S HOUSE - DAY

Ben is packing his things to leave. Alsi walks in.

                    ALSI
You are actually going to leave.

BEN

You better believe it my friend. A force is
about to hit the Delta only Mother Nature
could match. And as I have said before, I
want no parts of it.

ALSI

I really cannot believe what I am
witnessing. You are actually going to pack
up your family and move hundreds of miles
away, instead of defending your home.

BEN

(beat)
I left my home a long time ago. I am not
here to make the Nile Valley mines. I
simply came here to get a shear of its
world famous breadbasket.

ALSI

And what better opportunity is there to
get a share of this breadbasket.

BEN

This is not the way to get a shear in this
country. Since I have been here, I have
made more than sufficient to feed my
family, and I have never had to raise my
hand with arms against anyone.
(beat)
You are new here and have yet to see the
wrath of these Kushites, but I assure you
if you are here when the next landing
accrue, you will see terror your worst
nightmare could not produce.

ALSI

And still that does not frighten me to the
point where I would dare leave. I have
never had a fright from a dream that I
have not conquered.
(beat)
And I am not about to-

DADE

Father, father.

Dade runs in and grabs onto Ben's leg.

> DADE
> Marcus is making me pack to leave.

Marcus comes in too grab Dade.

> MARCUS
> Pardon us father.
> (to Dade)
> Come here you little rabbit.

Dade tightens his grip.

> DADE
> Noooooo.

> BEN
> Wait one moment Marcus.

Ben kneels down to explain to Dade.

> BEN
> It's alright son. Do as your brother says,
> the entire family is packing to leave.

> DADE
> We are? Where are we going?

> BEN
> We are all going to the village of Kurgus. It
> is no longer safe here, so we must leave.

> DADE
> Okay.
> (beat)
> Will Uncle Alsi and Cousin Srtife be coming
> also?

> BEN
> I am not sure.

Ben looks up at Alsi.

                    BEN
Why don't you ask him for yourself.

                    DADE
              (to Alsi)
Will you be coming with us also.

                    ALSI
              (off-guard)
Ahhh. Yes, I will be coming, but I won't be
leaving at the same time as the rest of the
family. There is something I must stay
behind and finish here first.

                    DADE
And when you are finished then will you
come and be with the rest of the family?

                    ALSI
I promise you when I am finish that will
be the first thing I do.

                    BEN
Okay, son now go with your brother and
start gathering your things to leave.

Dade and Marcus walk out together. Marcus kicks Dade in the ass. Ben and Alsi take
a beat.

                    BEN
Look I will no longer speak against you
wanting to fight for your share. Anything
that your heart desires, there's nothing I
would rather see than it becoming true for
you. But as for me, since this whole
confusion started, the innocent residents
of the Delta being offered refuge in Kurgus,
has been the only good news I have heard
thus far. And getting my family, as far away
from the Delta as possible, is all that I have
desired since Sting decided to join Beirut
and Kalili in any future war.

INT. SAIS - DAY

                    BEIRUT
                (to Kalili)
        You have requested to see me?

                    KALILI
        Yes. Our courier has returned. He have
        delivered our message and returned with
        a reply for us. The fighters will start
        arriving in two days.

EXT. FARM - DAY

It's a sunny day. Chief Narmer is riding. Along the way he passes a number of
FOREIGNERS from the Delta, migrating South to Kurgus. Narmer pays them no
attention. Narmer rides straight to a compound with a huge farm behind it.

EXT. FARM COMPOUND - DAY

Chief Narmer gives his horse to a HANDLER and walks to where the THIRD KEEPER
is waiting to greet him.

                    THIRD KEEPER
                (bows)
        Chief Narmer, welcome.

                    CHIEF NARMER
        Thank you. It has been a while since the
        last time I was here.

                    THIRD KEEPER
        Yes it has. My guards told me they
        recognized you riding up and I was so
        honored, I had to come and welcome you
        personally. So what brings you to these
        parts of the village?

                    CHIEF NARMER
        After the praise you gave to Djer at the
        last meeting of the order. I had to
        personally come and see his invention.

                    THIRD KEEPER
                (nods)
        You'll be very proud of him. He's a genius.

                    CHIEF NARMER
As of late it seems the entire village has
been telling me so.

                    THIRD KEEPER
They should, he deserves every praise.

Third Keeper turns to his Guard and says.

                    THIRD KEEPER
Go and fetch the Chief's son Djer.
          (to Narmer)
He will be with us shortly, perhaps he will
give you a personal demonstration and
explain all of his modifications.
          (beat)
Would you like some refreshments while
we wait?

                    CHIEF NARMER
No. Thank you.

                    THIRD KEEPER
So how was your trip?

                    CHIEF NARMER
It was pleasant, except for the migrating
Foreigners from the Delta heading to
Kurgus.

                    THIRD KEEPER
The number of Foreigners on their exodus
is increasing daily. If this keeps up, soon
there will be no foreign residents left in
the Delta. Soon they will all be relocated in
Kurgus.

                    CHIEF NARMER
Under any other circumstance I would
forbid it. But because of the current
situation, and they were invited by Chief
Duka, I will give them the benefit of the
doubt as the ones who had nothing to do
with the landings, and want nothing to do

with it. So I will over look it and allow
them to pass.

                    THIRD KEEPER
I agree with you they deserve the benefit
of the doubt, but knowing these Aliens,
these may very well be the same ones
responsible for the landings, and are now
just seizing this opportunity of being let
back into the south.

                    CHIEF NARMER
I myself have thought of that, but I must at
least-

A GUARD comes running toward them shouting.

                    GUARD
Keeper. Keeper.

                    THIRD KEEPER
This have better be important, that you
would dare interrupt me while I am
speaking with Chief Narmer.

                    GUARD
Pardon me Keeper, but it is because of
Chief Narmer being present why I am
interrupting you. Because I know he
would demand to know at once.

                    CHIEF NARMER
What is it that I would demand to know at
once?

                    GUARD
It's the Delta. There is a fleet of boats
docking as we speak. I just spotted them
through my viewer.

They follow behind the guard who leads them to the viewer. They stand in the
lookout tower, and look through the viewer toward the Delta region and the
Mediterranean Sea.

                    CHIEF NARMER
                (looks)
          I knew it, these Foreigners could never be
          trusted.

                    DJER
          What is going on?

                    CHIEF NARMER
          My son. I came here today to honor you, and
          witness your achievements in person. But...

He points to the viewer. Djer steps forward and take look through it.

                    CHIEF NARMER
          Now, I also have some trespassers that I
          must go and prepare to kill.

EXT. DOCK - DAY

Beirut and Kalili meet the FIGHTERS at the dock. There are five boats at the first
landing. TWO BRAVE-LOOKING MEN stand out from the rest. They exit the first two
boats. BEIRUT's GUARD introduces them to Beirut and Kalili.

                    BEIRUT's GUARD
          General these two men are the commanders
          of the fighters.

                    BEIRUT
                (to the guard)
          See to it that all the fighters get sufficient
          food, and rest to be revived of their
          strength.

                    BEIRUT'S GUARD
          Right away general.

The Guard walks off.

                    BEIRUT
                (to commanders)
          Gentlemen. I welcome you both to your
          paradise at last.

Beirut shakes their hands.

BEIRUT
I am General Beirut, and this is General
Kalili.

FIRST COMMANDER
General Beirut, General Kalili, it is an
honor to finally be in your presence. I am
First Commander. And this is Second
Commander, another member of our field
Generals.

SECOND COMMANDER
General Kalili, General Beirut, it is an
honor to serve men such as yourselves.
The old country praises you both for not
forgetting where your lineage comes from,
and for investing a portion of your wealth
into our countries young men, giving us
hope for the future.

KALILI
There is no reason to praise us. It is a part
of our patriotic duty in trying to build our
nation. But were we misinformed or were
the fighters supposed to be at least three
times this size.

FIRST COMMANDER
Yes General you were misinformed, the
fighters are actually five times the size of
what you see now. For strategic reasons we
have chosen to have five boats dock
everyday for the next five days.

BEIRUT
That was a very good idea. I am already
admiring the way your minds work.

FIRST LEADERS
Generals, we pledge to you both, one
hundred percent effort and loyalty for
giving us this opportunity. And we promise
you both, you will not be disappointed.

                    KALILI
It is very refreshing to hear that. I am
pleased to see you have both arrived with
your minds focused on strategy, as it needs
to be. If your fighters took that quality from
your leadership, this landing shall prove to
be very rewarding for us all very soon.

                FIRST COMMANDER
As I have said. We promise you will not be
disappointed.

                    BEIRUT
Well then my brothers, welcome to your
new home. Anything you may want,
whatever your hearts may desire, just you
ask. This is paradise. There is no wish that
will not be fulfilled.

                FIRST COMMANDER
Right now all I wish for is a seat that is not
moving, and a decent bowl of food.

                    BEIRUT
                   (laughs)
Certainly my friend.
                (to his Guard)
Guard.

Beirut's Guard runs over.

                BEIRUT'S GUARD
Yes General.

                    BEIRUT
See to it that the Commanders get our
finest quarters to rest in, and all the food
their eyes and taste buds desire.

                BEIRUT'S GUARD
I will personally see to it.

His Guard nods, walks off with the Commanders following close behind. Beirut
watches them leave.

                              BEIRUT
            This continues to look better for us, with
            every passing day.

                              KALILI
            Yes it does.
                    (beat)
            Now we must summons the rest of the
            Delta to Sais at once, and send Jusa his
            solicitation.

EXT. BUBA VILLAGE - DAY

Commotion in the town. PEOPLE hurrying around trying to leave. They are trying to
finish getting their belongings together. Ben puts his final load onto his horse.

                              BEN
            Has everyone put their loads onto the
            horses already?

                              BLOSSOM
            Yes, everyone load is on.

                              BEN
            Well. That is it then. Go and say your
            goodbyes.

Ben checks the hampers again to be sure they are secured on the horses. Blossom
and Ann walks over to Jaugen and Alsi to say goodbye.

                              BEN
            Children!

The three youngest sit together, waiting to leave. Srtife and Lena are off to the side,
not wanting to say goodbye. The children walk over to Ben, then over to Jaugen and
Alsi to say their farewells.

                              SRTIFE
                    (to Lena)
            I just cannot leave.

                              LENA
            Why not? Did you not say you wish to be
            with me?

                    SRTIFE
I do wish to be with you, but.
          (beat)
But I just cannot separate from my father
at this time.

                    LENA
Then I will stay here with you. I will go and
tell my father.

Lena tries to walk away, but Srtife stops her. Srtife holds her back.

                    SRTIFE
Wait. My love I wish you could stay here
with me. I enjoy your company so much I
selfishly am tempted to tell you that will
be wise. But your father would never allow
you to stay here in these circumstances.
And truth be told, he is doing the correct
thing, despite if our emotions are telling us
different.

Lena pulls away.

                    LENA
Well then let his no be the one that
prevents me from staying.

She goes over to her father.

                    LENA
Father.
          (beat)

                    BEN
What? What is it?

                    LENA
I wish to not travel to Kurgus with the rest
of the family. Instead, I wish to stay here
with Srtife.

                    BEN
          (sternly)
You make sure you hear me clear, because
I will not repeat myself. You say your

goodbyes and be mounted on your horse
and ready to leave by the time I walk back
over here. You think I have grown you to
this age to have you give your life away
foolishly. If Srtife wishes to be with you, he
will be able to find you in Kurgus.

Ben walks away headed over to Jaugen and Alsi. Srtife and Lena hug each other not
wanting to part ways. Ben's wives and children passes him as he walks over to Alsi,
Jaugen, and Jaugen's wife.

> BEN
> (to Jaugen and Alsi)
> Well my good friends. It seems as if this is
> where we part again.

> ALSI
> It seems so.
> (beat)
> It seems as if our life repeats the same
> cycle, no matter where we unite and call
> our home.

> BEN
> Let us hope the cycle continues to repeat
> itself. And we unite once again.

> ALSI
> We will cousin don't you fret. Just you be
> safe on your journey.

Ben shakes Alsi's hand.

> BEN
> I will. That will be no problem. Just you be
> sure to protect yourself through all of this
> confusion.

Ben turns to Jaugen who is hugging and kissing his wife. She is leaving with Ben and
the family. Ben shakes Jaugen's hand.

> BEN
> (to Jaugen)
> Jaugen my old friend, even though I just
> know some how you will make it out of

this situation safe, I beg of you to be
careful, ha.

                    JAUGEN
Don't you worry about me I am Fast
Jaugen. I have survived much worse than
this. Just you be sure to keep your family
out of harms way. I have grown quite fond
of them.

                    BEN
I will be sure to do so. My best wishes to
both you and Alsi.

                    ALSI
Thank you once again cousin for everything.

They all nod. Ben leaves. Rose kisses Jaugen then leaves behind Ben. They meet the rest of
the family at the horses.

Srtife kisses Lena goodbye. She gives him a necklace to remember her by. They hug and he
helps her onto her horse.

The family starts their journey, leaving Alsi, Jaugen, and Srtife behind watching them leave
until they disappear into the migrating crowds.

INT. NEKHEB MEETING HALL - DAY

The members of the council are assembling, getting ready for war.

                    KING SALO
It is obvious that these foreign invaders
have no intentions on stopping these
landings. So we will put a stop to it
ourselves.

                    COUNCIL
          (roars)
Yeaaa, We will teach them how. We will
put a stop to it for them. Etc.

                    N GUARD 1
          (shouts)
Generals, there's another set of boats
docking in the Delta as we speak.

The council member pause a beat in shock before they all heading to the balcony. Chief Narmer looks through the viewer.

                    CHIEF NARMER
          Well it is now obviously clear, these are
          no usual landings by the Foreigners. This
          is their third landing in as much days.
                    (beat)
          They are attacking the Empire.

                    FUSA
          This is good, let them come. I prefer killing
          them all at once anyway. Eradicate the
          entire strain and be rid of them once and
          for all.

                    CHIEF NARMER
                    (to Guard)
          Spread message throughout the Empire.
          Every Foreigner is forbidden to travel
          north. No exception. And get message to
          Chief Duka at Kurgus, tell him he have
          offer the so called innocent foreign
          population of the Delta refuge in his
          village, so he is now responsible for all of
          them. He is responsible for making sure
          there are no revolts from behind, by these
          Foreigners migrating south.

                    N GUARD 1
                    (nods)
          At once Chief.

The guard walks off, he passes Mnfeco as he arrives.

                    MNFECO
          Chief Narmer pardon me for being so late
          to arrive. I had to gather all my warriors.

                    CHIEF NARMER
          Mnfeco my brother you could never be late.
                    (jokingly)

Everyone in the Empire know that you would never let an adventure such as this miss you. Not in a million years.

                    MNFECO
          Not in a million years.
                    (beat)
          The Hierak warriors and I are here over
          seven thousand strong, ready to defend
          our Empire.

                    CHIEF NARMER
          The Empire is most grateful to have you
          and the Hierak Warriors here. The Ntchru
          will honor you.

                    MNFECO
          The opportunity to serve my Empire is
          more honor than I could ask for.

They nod to each other in respect. Mnfeco turns, and greets the rest of the council.

                    CHIEF NARMER
                    (to Fusa)
          Gather the rest of the Generals, and figure
          out what will be the best strategy to
          attack the Delta.
                    (beat)
          Also summon all the Babalu priests of the
          village to start the war ceremonial rituals.

Fusa nods, then leaves. Chief Narmer goes over to the other council memebrs, still looking through the viewer. Prince Chala and his General Hara stand off to the side. They nod in agreement and go their separate ways.

General Hara walks back over to join the other council members.

EXT. VILLAGES - DAY/NIGHT

Prince Chala rides his horse for two days nonstop. As the sun sets, and rises he is still riding. Prince Chala rides to the town of Sais.

EXT. SAIS - DAY

Prince Chala dresses in disguise as he makes his way through the town.

EXT. BEIRUT HOUSE - DAY

Prince Chala addresses Beirut's guard.

PRINCE CHALA
I'm here to see Beirut with a message
from Thebes.

The guard nods and walks inside.

INT. BEIRUT HOUSE - DAY

Beirut and Kalili are inside talking to the Delta leaders when the guard comes in.

FIRST COMMANDER
It is just that the fighters are growing more
anxious, with every passing moment.

BEIRUT
The battle will begin in due time. The
Kushites take time to gather themselves
for war. They weren't sitting with
knowledge of the landings waiting to
attack the Delta.

FIRST COMMANDER
If they are unprepared wouldn't it benefit
us if we attack them first.

BEIRUT
(frustrated)
Do you or your men know how to navigate
your way through the marshy lands of the
south. All your fighters have not even
arrived from the old country as yet.
(beat)
Anxiousness is a good character trait, but
often leads to ones down fall. Tell your
fighters to enjoy this time of peace, for
when the war begins they will wish they
had never seen the face of a Kushite.
(long beat)
And I assure you all, that time will be soon
enough.

BEIRUT'S GUARD
Pardon me General Beirut, but there is a
messenger from Thebes here to see you.

BEIRUT
(surprised)
A visitor from Thebes. Send him in.

The guard leaves to bring the messenger inside. Beirut and the other Delta leaders are surprised. The guard returns a disguised Prince Chala. Prince Chala says nothing.

KALILI
Did you not come here with a message?

He takes off the hood to reveal himself.

PRINCE CHALA
I have come with more than a message.

BEIRUT
Prince Chala, are you now delivering
messages for your uncle the King.

PRINCE CHALA
I am here for my own personal reasons,
and my uncle shall know nothing of this
visit.

BEIRUT
He shall never know, unless you reveal it.
(beat)
So what personal reasons have brought
you here to the Delta?

PRINCE CHALA
In my pursuit of my love, I am here to
seize an opportunity.
(beat)
You and I have had good trade relations
for a while now.

BEIRUT
Yes, we have.

PRINCE CHALA
And even though this is a time of mass
confusion. I am here with a proposition
that could benefit both the Delta, and
myself regardless of how this confusion
plays out.

KALILI
Exactly what do you have in mind?

PRINCE CHALA
Nowhere in the Empire is it not known
that, the only reason King Salo has not yet
named his successor is because Chief
Narmer has not accepted. He has
continuously overlooked me, his own flesh
and blood, the prince, the rightful heir. For
this man who seems to think he is here to
save the Empire. And I promise you if
Narmer comes back successful from this
campaign, the people of the Empire will
give him the crown. And by that point it
will be too late for him to decline.

KALILI
Are you here to complain about the
Empire's personal affairs? Or are you here
with a proposition.

PRINCE CHALA
When the Empire comes to the Delta to
carry out their promise of the
proclamation, see to it that Chief Narmer
does not leave the Delta alive. And I will be
in your favor when I am crowned King.

KALILI
If the Empire attacks us, what makes you
feel that any Kushites will be leaving the
Delta alive?

PRINCE CHALA
(laughs)
I wonder what is it that have gotten you all
so over zealous, is it the fifteen to twenty
boats that have landed. Or do you
Foreigners just like the feeling of danger?

KALILI
Actually, a little of both.

PRINCE CHALA

Though the landings over the past couple
of days probably have your testicles
feeling bigger. I could assure you it would
take no more than five village's warriors to
kill every occupant in the Delta. My advises
to you is to stay alive, because when the
Empire gets here death will be your
companion, and staying alive will be your
only victory.

BEIRUT

And what makes you think that you will be
crowned King, if Chief Narmer gets killed.

PRINCE CHALA

Because I am the rightful heir. If it were
not for my uncle's fondness of Narmer, he
would not even be an option. Me coming
back alive, and Chief Narmer not, that is all
it would take.

BEIRUT

And how are we to know that you 'll make
it back alive.

PRINCE CHALA

That will also be a part of our agreement.

Prince Chala shows them his emblem.

PRINCE CHALA

Any of the Empire's warriors wearing my
royal emblem is not to be harmed. These
significant others, and myself will be
fighting specifically to secure my crown.
Not to carry out Narmer's proclamation
against the Delta.

KALILI

And what favor are we to expect from you
in return.

PRINCE CHALA

When I am crowned King, just name it
and it shall be done.

They shake hands.

> BEIRUT
> Prince Chala we accept your proposition.

INT. GREETING HALL AT NEKHEB - DAY

Chief Narmer greets the Empire's WARRIORS. He talks with Chief Bobo who has just arrived.

> CHIEF NARMER
> I thank you for living up to the reputation of our great ancestral city of Meroe, and coming to defend our Empire.

> CHIEF BOBO
> Chief Narmer I have been killing foreign men before you were born. And as of late I have been longing for some of my youthful experiences.

> CHIEF NARMER
> (smiles)
> Well my brother, it seems father time has came back around, to give you another youthful thrill ride.

> CHIEF BOBO
> Yes he has. And I am looking forward to making this the thrill of my life. The Meroe warriors and I are here over thirteen thousand strong, eager to get into the thick of it.

> CHIEF NARMER
> The Generals are gathered together now as we speak, coming up with a unified strategy. Don't you worry your adventure will begin soon.

> BERENIB
> Good day to you Chief Bobo. I do not mean to intrude, but may I speak with my husband for a moment.

CHIEF BOBO

And a Good day to you also chief wife
Berenib. You certainly may. Go right ahead.
I must go and catch up with the other
Chiefs and Generals, so that I can take part
in the remainder of the war ceremonies.

CHIEF NARMER

Okay then. We will catch up at the war
ceremony.

Bobo nods and leaves. Chief Narmer turns to Bereib.

CHIEF NARMER

What is it that you wish to speak with me
about my love.

BERENIB

The women of the village have been
meeting, trying to see what could we do in
these times, to show our support to the
Empire.

CHIEF NARMER

Really. And what have you all come up
with.

BERENIB

We have decided that us women will
continue the labor that had to be put on
hold by the men, who have answered the
call to war. We will see to it that the
affairs of the Empire continue to be
carried out with no interruptions.

CHIEF NARMER

That's very admirable of our women. The
Empire needs all the support and sacrifice
we could get.

BERENIB

We have already sent messages to the
women of the other villages of the Empire.
We figured in this time of war, it is the
least we could do to show our support.

CHIEF NARMER
I respect that very much my love, and I am
sure all the other warriors of the Empire
will also.

BERENIB
Also, Tifa have gathered together roughly
three hundred women from Nekheb, who
want to show their support by way of
fighting.

CHIEF NARMER
(giggles, reject)
What? There is no need for our women to
join a physical battle. We have more than
enough warriors for that.

BERENIB
She is aware of that. But for the past five
days, we have all sat and watched boats
dock every day with the arrival of more
and more foreign invaders. We are all just
trying to do what we can to help, and
fighting is where Tifa and these specific
women feel they could be the most helpful.

CHIEF NARMER
I am not surprise to hear such an offer
from Tifa. She's always been strapping
enough to brawl with any man. But where
did she find three hundred women willing
to fight.

BERENIB
Right here in Nekheb. The majority of the
Empires women feel just as strongly
about the dockings as our men.

CHIEF NARMER
Well, knowing Tifa I won't be able to talk
her out of this, if her mind has already been
made up.
(beat)
So I 'll tell you what I will do. I will allow
them to fight under General Fusa, or
whomever he puts in command of them.

                    BERENIB
I am sure that will be good enough for
Tifa. She only wants the honor of serving
her Empire.

                CHIEF NARMER
Okay then. They are more than welcome
to serve.

                    BERENIB
                (nods gratefully)
The women of the Empire thanks you my
Chief.

Berenib pauses to console Narmer as his wife.

                    BERENIB
So how are you doing my love, how are
you feeling?

                CHIEF NARMER
I am fine, just a little tired. I have not slept
in the past four nights.

Berenib massages her husband's neck.

                    BERENIB
You might as well start getting use to it.
Sleepless nights are a part of being a
productive King.

He takes her by the hand and sits her on his lap.

                CHIEF NARMER
What are you talking about?

                    BERENIB
Who do you think, every single individual
person, in the Empire gives credit for
taking a stance against the Delta? And even
more important what do you think is going
to happen when you come back victorious?

Duba walks in, and interrupts them.

                              DUBA
Pardon me, Chief Narmer and the Chief
Wife Berineb. Am I interrupting you two?

                            BERENIB
Awe. No you are not.

Berenib kisses Narmer and whispers in his ear.

                            BERENIB
The people of the Empire will be offering
you the crown this time.

She leaves. Her eyes are locked with Narmer's eyes. Narmer sits back in a daze.

                            BERENIB
                          (to Duba)
Hello.

She leaves. Duba walks over to Narmer.

                              DUBA
Greetings Chief Narmer, I have just
arrived with over three thousand Aswan
warriors, ready to defend the Empire.

                        CHIEF NARMER
Chief Duba, the highest of respect to you,
and the Aswan warriors for even showing
up, considering everything that your
people has been through recently.

                              DUBA
Honestly, if it were for any other cause, I
probably would not even have come here
today. But the dockings are something I
am very opposed to, and would have
taken this stance on my deathbed.

                        CHIEF NARMER
Well this is something else that it seems
we both-

                              POPA
Greetings Chief Narmer. Chief Duba.

Chief Popa comes up from behind.

>   CHIEF NARMER
> Chief Popa. I did not see you come in.
> Welcome.
>   (beat)
> I,m glad you have made it to join us. After
> the last council meeting, I was not sure if
> we would see you here to support the
> Empire on this issue.

>   POPA
> At the last council meeting, I did not think
> I would be here either. But over the past
> couple of days, my point of view has
> changed about a lot of things.

>   CHIEF NARMER
> That is just a part of life. Our point of view
> often changes with the times. I am just
> glad those changes have led you here
> today.

>   POPA
> Yes they have, and I am here with the
> Kerman warriors over five thousand
> strong. Pledging our support to the
> Empire.

>   CHIEF NARMER
> Your Empire thanks you.

>   POPA
>   (apologizes)
> Also I would like to apologize to you if I-

>   CHIEF NARMER
> My brother all of that is already forgotten.
>   (beat)
> This is a time for brotherhood. We have a
> war ceremony to get to, so let us go and
> enjoy our-selves, and catch up with the
> rest of the council.

They walk off together with Duba, headed to the war ceremony where the entire
Empire is celebrating. It's a stereotypical African gathering.

EXT. WAR CEREMONY AT NEKHEB - DAY

SOME PEOPLE are chanting and dancing around campfires, SOME are making weapons OTHERS are practice against each other. The BABALU PRIESTS are sacrificing animals and performing their customs war rituals.

WARRIORS are everywhere talking, joking, quarreling, drinking, smoking, and having a good time.

Chief Narmer, Popa, and Duba pass through to the other Chiefs and Generals.

The Generals are in the middle of acting out their war strategy. Fusa notices them coming and goes over to greet them.

                    FUSA
              (bows)
         Welcome Chief Duba, Chief Popa.

                    POPA
              (nods)
         General Fusa, It is an honor to be here.

                    DUBA
              (nods)
         I would not miss this for anything on
         Earth.

                    FUSA
         I know the people of the Empire thanks
         you both for coming.
              (to Chief Narmer)
         You all have arrived just in time. We are
         in the middle of going over our strategies.

                    CHIEF NARMER
         I am pleased to hear that, what have you
         and the other Generals come up with.

                    FUSA
         Let me have the demonstrators,
         demonstrate for you.

Fusa CLAPS loudly to stop the demonstration.

Start over once again from the beginning, and
demonstrate for Chief Narmer, Chief Duba,
and Chief Popa who has just arrived.

The demonstrators get back into positions and start from the top. They perform the
war stratagem as General Fusa's explains it to Narmer.

FUSA
The other Generals and I have decided on
probably our most basic strategy ever. We
have decided to divide the twelve village's
warriors into three units, for three separate
waves of attack. And because of the fact that
we are going to take back the entire Delta! As
we push north, we will conquer every village
along the way. We have already gotten word,
that there are no foreign fighters South of
Sais, so we shouldn't meet any resistance
until then. But never the less, in our first
wave of infantry we will send enough
warriors to conquer everything along the
way, and the Delta if need be. The first wave
will consist of the Madjai long range bow and
arrow marks men, the long spear horse men
to ram there front line, and also short spear
and sword men for the close hand to hand
combat. We will sail north up the Nile, with a
Calvary of horsemen on the East and West
Bank of the Nile accompanying us. When we
come in contact with the foreign invaders, we
will line up in attempt to draw them out into
their fighting formation. Once they are lined
up our Madjai long-range bow and arrow
marksmen, will start raining down arrows
from afar, injuring a substantial amount of
their fighters as we advance forward. Once
we are close enough, our long spear
horsemen will charge them. Ramming down,
and breaking through their front line, which
should separate, and confuse them. Making
way for our hand-to-hand warriors to come
in and finish them off. The first wave will
press and conquer everything as far as Buba,
there they will wait, sound the drums, and
send message to notify the other two units to

come to Buba. Upon the reinforcements
arrival a second unit will join and strengthen
the first, resupplying them with weapons and
men power if necessary. Them together they
take Sais, while the third unit waits in Buba
close behind as reinforcement and protection
from the Foreigners who have traveled south
to Kurgus just in case of an attack from
behind.

CHIEF NARMER
It sounds good enough to me simple and
straight to the point.
        (to the leaders)
And do all of us standing here as brothers
of the Kushite Empire, feel satisfied with
this strategy.

GENERALS AND CHIEFS
        (various)
Yes we do. We are satisfied with it.

CHIEF NARMER
Then so it is. We ride out to take the Delta
at first light.

The crowd erupts.

CHIEF NARMER
But tonight let us awake the Ka energy of
our Ntchru Mother Nun the virgin mother
and her chosen Sun our father of light, the
greater light Atun Ra, who gives us life and
guide us throughout the day. And their
vibration Patah the vibration of creation
who likewise gives us life by lifting us up
out of the waters which is the fullness there
of. Let us make sacrifices and sing praises
unto them, so that our covenant will not be
forgotten. Let us honor them so that they
will be with us on the battlefield, so that
they will be our strength, our spear, and
our shield.

The Chiefs and Generals erupt in cheers, then chants. They dance and sing in joy.

Five Babalu Priests are in a deep trance, praying over the Chiefs and Generals in a circle. The Priests place a necklace for protection on all the Chiefs and Generals.

Outside the circle are four altars with animals being sacrificed. The blood is smeared over the Chiefs and Generals, then everyone else.

The Kushites dance around fires in deep trances, while they chant and sing engulfed in their custom ritual.

EXT. READY FOR WAR AT NEKHEB - MORNING

The war ceremonies continue into the morning of the War. It's dusk. The entire Kushite Empire is awake and ready for war. The Chiefs and General are on horsebacks, huddled together in a final meeting.

Through the mist and smoke, a WARRIOR notices Tifa and her posse riding up.

The Chiefs and Generals glance over to see what's the cause of the commotion. The WARRIORS start to make jokes and sexist remarks. Tifa and posse ride through proudly, not paying any attention to the hecklers.

Tifa and posse head straight towards Chief Narmer.

> WARRIORS
> Women coming dressed prepared for
> war, now I have seen it all. Have one of
> your husbands left home without
> permission, and now you all are here to
> teach him a lesson.

They continue taunting.

> WARRIORS
> A woman place is in the home not at war.
> Here he is, here is the man that has
> impregnated your daughter.

> MNFECO
> (to the other Leaders)
> What on earth has gotten into these
> women?

> CHIEF NARMER
> They are here to fight for their Empire.

FUSA
What could have given them the
impression that they are needed to fight
for the Empire.

CHIEF NARMER
I did.

Everyone looks at him.

FUSA
Why would you do such a thing, they are
not needed.

The crowd still taunts. Tifa ignores them.

TIFA
Good morning to you King Salo, and to
you Chief Narmer. The same to all you
Chiefs and Generals! The women of
Nekheb and I are here to pledge our
support to the Empire.

CHIEF NARMER
And a good morning to you Tifa.

KING SALO
Yes, a very good morning to you warrior
princes. The bravery of you and these
female warriors is most impressive.
Especially when this campaign does not
call for such a sacrifice.

TIFA
These women and I only wish to do our
shear for the Empire in the area we feel
we could be the most helpful.

The crowd laughs.

CROWD
What's the matter ladies, you all have not
gotten any good loving in a long time. I
could be of help, but I cannot satisfy all of
you.

The crowd laughs again.

                    KING SALO
          The pledge from you and all these brave
          women is greatly respected. I look
          forward to hearing about you all in the
          thick of it. This Empire has always had
          great Warrior Princesses whom are
          legendary in battle.

                    CHIEF NARMER
               (to Tifa)
          I will be with you shortly to brief you on
          the chain of command.

Narmer turns to talk to the circle of Chiefs and Generals.

                    CHIEF NARMER
          I know this is not what any of you had in
          mind, but I am asking one of you to please
          let them ride under your command.

                    FUSA
          Are you serious? You are actually going to
          allow them fight.

                    CHIEF NARMER
          I have already promised them. Plus what
          harm could it do.

                    FUSA
          Women riding into battle is completely
          unnecessary. We have more than enough
          warriors.

                    CHIEF NARMER
          I 'm aware of that.
               (beat)
          Look the point is they are here to show
          their support. Which one of you wants to
          be the one to go over there, and tell Tifa
          you will not allow her to fight?

They all pause for a moment, then lift up their heads to look at Tifa who looks like a
true warrior.

KING SALO
There is no reason to deny them. Surely
one of you could let them ride alongside
you to feel useful, while making sure you
keep them out of harm's way.

CHIEF NARMER
(to Fusa)
Would that be something that you would
be able to do.

FUSA
That will be impossible. I like you will be
on the front line. I have no time to tend to
a woman.

DUBA
Chief Narmer, I will be in the second wave.
And if it is all the same, they could ride
alongside the Aswan warriors.

CHIEF NARMER
It is all the same to me.
(beat)
Okay then we all know our duties. Gather
your warriors and prepare to ride out.

The circle of Generals and Chiefs separates and everyone goes over to their village
warriors. Chief Duba and Narmer ride over to Tifa. King Salo rides over to Prince
Chala's General Hara.

KING SALO
General Hara, how are the Throne warriors?

GENERAL HARA
They are all armored up and ready to ride
my King.

KING SALO
That is good. Where is Prince Chala, I have
not seen him in the past three days. Has he
decided not to accompany the Empire on
this campaign?

GENERAL HARA
He should be along shortly my King. He
left for home three nights ago saying it
was most urgent.

The King nods and moves on. Djer is with the Kushite warriors lined up. They all
have weapons in hand, some on horseback, others on foot. They all marching to the
Nile River viciously.

The Chiefs and General are in the front of the procession. They march through the
town with the women and children looking on.

EXT. NILE RIVER - DAY

The Empire's warriors reach the Nile where fleets of boats await them. Chief
Narmer looks at the King and nods, pleased. The warriors get into formation.

Prince Chala rides onto the scene. The first wave is ready to go, with Chief Mnfeco on
the East bank with a set of warriors under his command. Chief Narmer on a boat
with Djer, and a fleet of boats with warriors under his command. General Fusa on
the West bank with a set of warriors under his command.

Prince Chala comes over, and rides alongside Fusa. The first wave pushes North
towards the Delta.

The REINFORCEMENTS watch with the locals. They locals wave goodbye to the first
wave.

INT. SAIS VILLAGE - DAY

The Delta leaders are relaxing when a MESSENGER runs up and tells them.

MESSENGER
The Kushites are on the move, and are
now making there way north.

Everyone stands.

FIRST COMMANDER
Finally the time has come.

KWAME
(to Donoe)
I wish I was none the wiser like these new
comers, and had no idea of what is
coming.

DONOE
                         Not knowing does not make them any safer.
                         I think we have an advantage because we
                         do know what is coming. So my advice to
                         you is to fall back and let them with their
                         eagerness rush out first to weaken the
                         Kushites.

Beirut puts on a protective vest.

                         BEIRUT
                         Okay men, the Kushites are on their way,
                         so let us prepare to fight for the greater
                         good of freedom, and all the privileges that
                         comes with the honor.

The room cheers.

                         BEIRUT
                         So let us slay these Kushites. Take our
                         privilege and honor. And take control of
                         our future.

The crowd erupts. Everyone parts ways. Sting walks over to brief his Buban fighters.
He passes Jaugen and Alsi on the way.

Jaugen is trying to con a NEWCOMER out of something. The newcomer doesn't fall
for it, and walks over to First Commander who is addressing his fighters. Jaugen
then turns around to hear what Sting is saying.

Suddenly loud cheers start erupting from the different groups of Delta fighters.

EXT. NILE RIVER - CONTINUOUS

The Empire Warriors head North, Chief Narmer on the Nile, Mnfeco on the East
bank, and Fusa on the West bank. They all look fearless.

Some of the foreign population heading south to Kurgus, pass the Empire's warriors
headed north to the Delta. The Kushites stop them and take them as prisoners and
continue combing each village as they go along.

The warriors stops Ben's family along the way, but Ben is not with them.

The warriors get to Athra and Narmer gives the commands.

CHIEF NARMER
Warriors of the Kushite Empire, we all
know what we must do. I want no stone
unturned. Seize, and round up every
individual in the city. They are all now
officially prisoners of the Kushite Empire.
If any of you should meet any resistance
while carrying out your duty, do not
hesitate to kill.

The Warriors let out a loud cry to motivate themselves. The Empire's warriors
charge into Athra.

EXT. ATHRA - DAY

The Warriors run through the village destroying everything in their way. Shops,
houses, and buildings. They comb the village and find no one.

They destroy, and burn the town. Narmer, Fusa, and Mnfeco go back to the Nile, and
prepare to head further north to Buba.

Before leaving for Buba, Narmer sends message back to the other units.

EXT. BUBA - DAY

The Empire's warriors push north, and reach Buba. They charge the village just as
they did at Athra. They raid, destroy, and burn but once again the village is already
abandoned.

EXT. SAIS MEETING HALL - DAY

Beirut sits amongst the other leaders in the Sais meeting hall. A MESSENGER walks
in and notifies him.

Beirut nods then stands to address everyone.

BEIRUT
Fighters for freedom, our time has come.
Prepare to defend yourselves. The
Kushites are close. They are just south of
us at Buba. The entire village is burning.

The Delta fighters stop what they are doing and start arming them-selves.

BEIRUT
Let us not forget our strategy, and stick to
it. As we have agreed, we will split up into
two groups. One will stay behind in the
center of the town, while the other push
forward onto the battlefield. We will trick
the Kushites into thinking that is all our
fighters. When they attack, we will put up
a small resistance, to make it seems as if
we are standing our ground, but in
actuality we will be retreating backwards
into the town, making it look as if we are
overwhelmed. The Kushites will then get
over confident, pursue us into the interior
of the town, where our awaiting fighters
will ambush them.

The fighters let out a loud CHEER and raise their weapons.

EXT. BUBA VILLAGE - DAY

Narmer and the first wave of warriors are at Buba waiting. They're relaxing while
waiting for the backup units.

The town is still burning behind them as the warriors are laughing, eating, and
roasting animals.

Narmer, Fusa, Mnfeco, Prince Chala, and the other Generals and Chiefs are all
together eating.

Through the smoke emerges Chief Duba and the other Generals and Chiefs with
reinforcement. The Mumon General Masa and some Mumon warriors have now
joined the Empire's effort. Narmer and the other Generals and Chiefs stand to greet
them as they ride over.

DUBA
Greetings Chief Narmer we have received
your message. Were there any resistances
here in Buba?

CHIEF NARMER
None what so ever, it seems our informants
were correct. They are all waiting at Sais.

DUBA
It makes no difference where they are
waiting. They will have nowhere to run.

The Mumon General Masa walks toward them.

DUBA
(sarcastically)
Look who has decided to come along and
join us.

GENERAL MASA
Greetings Chief Narmer, pardon us for
arriving so late. It took us awhile to
gather enough warriors, who were
healthy enough to be of any assistance to
this campaign.

CHIEF NARMER
Considering the current status of your
people, the Empire admires the Mumons
strength just for making it here.

GENERAL MASA
Though things are difficult for the Mumon
village at the moment, we are still a part of
this Empire and must defend it.

CHIEF NARMER
Your Empire respect and honor the
Mumon commitment.

They shake hands.

GENERAL MASA
The privilege to serve this Empire is all the
honor the Mumon village need.

CHIEF NARMER
(to Duba)
See to it that the warriors that have just
arrived with you are fed and rested. Also
make sure the four tribes, which will join
us on the campaign, are ready to ride. We
take Sais at first light.

DUBA
Consider it done, Chief Narmer.

Duba walks off to go see to it. Narmer sits back down. Zomi and the other Generals and Chiefs walk over and greet Narmer.

EXT. BUBA VILLAGE - NEXT DAY

The night passes and at sunrise, the Kushite Empire's warriors are mounted, and ready to attack Sais.

Narmer and the other leaders are huddled in a circle going over their strategies. They break, and take their positions.

Narmer, who still leads his unit from the Nile, gives the Empire's warriors the signal to push north.

Djer is still with his father's unit. The third wave stays behind in Buba as reinforcement and protection to prevent any attacks from behind.

The Kushites push north to Sais after doubling their numbers in warriors, now looking fiercer and deadlier than ever.

EXT. SAIS VILLAGE - DAY

Beirut walks out onto a balcony to address the Delta fighters.

BEIRUT
My brothers in arm, the Kushites are now
on their way to Sais. Let us ready our-
selves and get into formation. Let us stand
our ground together. Stick to our strategy.
And the future will be ours.

The Delta fighters let out a LOUD CHEER. They grab their weapons and get into formation.

Jaugen, Alsi, and Srtife are amongst all the cheering. They march with the other foreign fighters into an open field, and start lining up. Beirut mounts his horse.

EXT. SAIS VILLAGE - DAY

Narmer and the Kushite warriors are on their way to the heart of Sais, when they see the Delta fighters lined up in the distance.

The Kushites continue to move forward. The Delta fighters spot the Kushites, and stand their ground.

Narmer positions the Empire's warriors where he wants them. He halts the warriors to give them a final command.

>   CHIEF NARMER
>   (raises his hand)
>   Warriors of the Kushite Empire, we know
>   the reason why we are here. Every Alien
>   in our way is to be killed. If they are still
>   here in the Delta, their desire is to over
>   throw our Empire. So to any foreign face
>   you come across, have no mercy. Let us
>   rid ourselves of these invading foreign
>   parasites once and for all.

The Kushite Warriors start cheering and pushes forward again. The Delta fighters see the Kushites coming, but stand their ground as planned.

Chief Narmer is now on shore, commanding as they move in closer. When the Kushite Warriors get close enough, Narmer gives the order and the Madjaies begin to shoot arrows from a distance.

The Delta fighters begin shooting arrows back, but with no real affect.

The Kushite Madjaies are seasoned marksmen. From the Nile, the east, and the west bank on Narmer's command, the Kushite Madjaies make arrows rain down on the Delta fighters.

On every command Narmer has two sets of shooters, one shoots in the air letting the arrow fall from the sky, while the other shooters shoots straight. So if the Delta fighters try to block high they get hit low, and if they try to block low, they get hit high.

Meanwhile the Delta shooters aren't doing much damage to the Kushites. Beirut and Kalili notice, and starts telling the Delta fighters to move back, even before the Kushites charge.

>   BEIRUT
>   Fall back! Fall back! Get out of the range
>   of their arrows.

>   STING
>   We cannot retreat. They have not charged
>   us as yet.

                    BEIRUT
          We are not retreating only moving out of
          the range of their arrows. Can't you see
          that they are already injuring too many of
          our fighters, without using any real effort.

They stare at each other. Sting is reluctant, but rides to the front line and tells the
Delta fighters to fall back.

The Kushites keep firing steadily as they watch the Delta fighters slowly retreat. The
Kushites erupt in cheers.

                  CHIEF NARMER
                    (to Fusa)
          Look at them, already running like the
          cowards they are. Let us charge in and
          finish them, while we have them on the
          run.

The Empire's warriors continue to cheer, and shout arrows at the retreating Delta
fighters.

                    FUSA
          We cannot charge them as yet. They are
          still at full strength. We have done no real
          damage to their fighters as yet. Nearly
          thirty ships landed in the Delta that was
          not even a half of their passengers. Them
          retreating could easily be a trap.

                  CHIEF NARMER
          It makes no difference if it is. They are
          running frightened, and confused. Let us
          not give them the opportunity to get into
          position, and maneuver that trap.

                  PRINCE CHALA
          Even if they have a trap set, they cannot
          over power our numbers. And like Chief
          Narmer said, if we keep them running
          frightened and confused, there is no way
          they 'll be able to execute it properly.

Chief Narmer pauses for a beat. He looks at the fleeing Delta fighters and points,
signaling an attack. He then SCREAMS it at the top of his lungs.

CHIEF NARMER
ATTAAAAAAAACK

The Kushites charge after the fleeing Delta fighters chasing behind them like predator chasing its prey. Arrows are still flying back and forth, with people still getting killed.

Beirut notices that the Kushite warriors are charging behind them, and begins ordering the Delta fighters to get back inside the compound.

BEIRUT
(to Donoe)
They are charging us, get all the fighters
back inside the compound. EVERYONE
BACK INSIDE THE COMPOUND.
EVERYONE BACK INSIDE THE
COMPOUND.

DONOE
Everyone back inside the compound.
Everyone back inside the compound.

All the other Delta leaders notice and follow.

OTHER LEADERS
Everyone back inside the compound.

The fighters all head back to the center of town and barricade themselves inside the compound, with the Kushites still in pursuit.

Once the Kushite warriors get to the interior of the town, they begin receiving shots from Delta fighters hiding on the top of buildings.

The Kushites try to fight their way out of it. The Kushite warriors take cover and shoot back, while losing a significant amount of warriors.

When Kalili notices the plan is working, Kalili gives the signal to two of the LANDING COMMANDERS on rooftops to attack. Suddenly from in front and behind the Kushite Warriors two doors fly open, with two Delta units charging out at them to do more damage.

Mnfeco notices.

MNFECO
Look out, they are charging us from behind.

CHIEF NARMER
Now this is how I like it, at least send a
few out to fight. You all cannot be
cowards running, and hiding behind
barricades.

Narmer and Mnfeco begin the killing, as the Delta fighters charge out at them. The two armies battle on, with the Delta seeming to have the upper hand for the moment, thanks to their shooters on the rooftops.

Duba starts shooting fire arrows onto the rooftops, to try and burn out the Delta fighters. All of the Empire's Leaders are holding their-own during the battle.

Narmer is killing everything in his way, Zomi is killing everything in his way, Mnfeco is slewing them, Duba is slewing them, Fusa is slewing them, Tifa is slewing them, Djer is slewing them.

Even Prince Chala and General Masa are acting like they are slewing them, while looking for their opportunity to disrupt the Empire's effort.

Meanwhile the Delta fighters are still shooting arrows from rooftops, killing a substantial amount of Kushite warriors.

Kalili notices that the Kushites are still standing their ground, so he orders four more units to charge. Two more doors fly open on one side of the compound, and two more on another, and more Foreign Fighters come charging out at the Kushite warriors.

This time the Delta fighters are led by two more of the landing commanders, plus Sting, and Donoe.

The fighters get to the Kushites and unleash their fury. Narmer is in the middle of the combat killing every Foreigner in his way.

Jaugen, Alsi, and Srtife come charging out with Sting, and they are holding their own. Donoe is holding his own for an old man. The two landing commanders are holding their own also, showing their exceptional fighting skills.

The two armies are going at each other in deadly combat, Foreigners killing natives and natives killing Foreigners.

Jaugen, Alsi, and Srtife are in the middle of the combat holding their own, while watching each other's back.

Beirut and the Sais fighters are still shooting arrows from their compound rooftops, while Duba is still ordering the Empire's warriors to shoot fire arrows back at the Delta fighters on the rooftops.

Fusa is in the middle of ramming the compound gate, trying to get inside. Fusa screams the orders as he shoots arrows at the fighters on the roofs.

FUSA

Again! Again!

Fusa is determined to protect the Empire's warriors ramming the gate. The Kushites are beginning to counter the Delta's attack by climbing onto rooftops, and by breaking down all the courtyard doors, trying to prevent any more charges.

Young Djer, and Tifa are still holding their own.

Then all of a sudden, Prince Chala's General Hara, in the middle of fighting sneakily turns around and shoots the Hierak village General Ourou in the back, then turns back around and continues fighting without being noticed.

General Ourou kills his opponent then falls to one knee, and turns around to see who shot him, but sees nobody.

General Ourou bears the pain, and breaks the arrow, then stands back up enraged and continues fighting.

Fusa is still ramming the gate, and it is getting weaker, plus Duba and the Aswan warriors are still shooting fire arrows, which are beginning to pay off.

The Sais compound is steadily catching afire. The Delta fighters are trying but cannot put out all the flames fast enough. More and more Kushite warriors have gotten onto the rooftops penetrating the Delta's defense.

Meanwhile Chief Bobo is slewing everything in his way, when he comes across Donoe. They spot each other.

BOBO
(to Donoe)
Old man Donoe, the great deceiver of the
Delta. Why don't you tell me one of those
clever alibis and lets see will my sword
pardon you.

                    DONOE
Chief Bobo you have already been
deceived. And you calling me old only
prove that you still have not face reality.

                    BOBO
The only reality I will acknowledge is my
sword separating you limb by limb.

                    DONOE
Once again you still have not faced reality.

This upsets Bobo and he charges Donoe. They square off.

Their weapon of choice is the sword. They fight for a while, with nobody seeming to
have the upper hand, when Bobo gives Donoe a cut. They pause and Donoe takes a
look at his cut, and gets upset.

Donoe gets aggressive, and starts chopping away at Bobo wildly, but Bobo easily
blocks them all holding his own.

Then all of a sudden from behind, Bobo gets hit with an arrow in the back.

Donoe pauses to see who shot it. It was one of the Mumon traitors. Donoe stays on
the attack, trying to take advantage of the situation.

Bobo gets weaker, and it becomes harder for him to block Donoe chops.

Donoe starts getting a few cuts in, injuring Bobo seriously, then Donoe eventually
gets Bobo down and to the point where Donoe is about to finish Bobo.

Djer spots them across the way, and fires an arrow straight through Donoe's hand
before he could deliver the deathblow to Bobo. Djer realizes he has injured Donoe,
and rides over to save Chief Bobo. Djer rides over, jumps off his horse, and attacks
Donoe while Donoe is still tending to his hand.

Djer and Donoe begin fighting while Bobo lie on the ground injured, in agony
watching them fight.

Djer is holding his own, but the older, and more experienced Donoe seems to have
the upper hand.

Bobo is still watching them fight when Bobo notice an arrow flying pass barely
missing Djer's head.

Bobo turns to see who it came from, and notices a Mumon warrior cocked, aimed, and ready to shoot again.

Bobo quickly reaches for his bow and arrow, and kills the Mumon traitor before the traitor could get off another shot.

Chief Bobo then slumps back down in pain.

Meanwhile Donoe is wearing down Djer, but fighting right next to them is Tifa who has just finished killing the man she was fighting.

Tifa then turns around and helps Djer. They both double team Donoe, get the upper hand, and starts wearing Donoe down. Then together Tifa and Djer kill Donoe.

They then rush over to Chief Bobo, to see if he is still alive. Djer kneels over Chief Bobo.

                    DJER
          Chief Bobo, are you O.K.

                    BOBO
               (gasping for air)
          The arrow head is deep inside of me, I can
          hardly breathe, but I will be fine. The
          Mumon warriors, they did this to me.

                    DJER
          What?

                    BOBO
          Yes, they must have come here to betray
          the Empire. You must warn the rest of the
          Empire's warriors.

Bobo finishes telling them then slumps back down in pain. Tifa and Djer looks at each other shocked cannot believe it, then turn to look for any signs of it being true.

Right away they see a Mumon warrior take aim, and fire an arrow killing Chief Rasa's and the Napata village General Bongo.

Djer stands up and fires an arrow, hitting the Mumon traitor directly in the chest. Before the traitor dies he noticed that Djer was the one who shot him, and points Djer and Tifa out to another Mumon traitor.

The other Mumon traitor takes aim, and starts shooting arrows rapidly at Djer and Tifa. Tifa pulls Chief Bobo out of the way, and they both take cover.

Djer starts running, and has to dive behind some baskets stacked on top of each other to avoid getting hit.

Djer then rises up, and sends back an arrow, forcing the Mumon traitor to take cover.

Djer disappears into the crowd shouting to the Kushite warriors that the Mumons are here to betray the Empire.

> DJER
> (shouts)
> THE MUMONS ARE HERE TO BETRAY
> THE EMPIRE. THE MUMONS ARE HERE
> TO BETRAY THE EMPIRE.

Djer disappears amongst all the fighting.

Meanwhile more and more Kushite warriors have gotten onto rooftops, and are battling the Delta fighters. Duba and his unit's fire arrows have almost three quarters of the Sais compound ablaze, plus Fusa is still ramming the gate and the gate is about to give.

The Sais guard tells Beirut that the gate will no longer hold, so Beirut decides to charge out and fight.

> BEIRUT'S GUARD
> (shouts)
> General the gate will no longer hold.

> BEIRUT
> Prepare the fighters, to open the gate and
> attack.

Beirut and all the other Delta leaders mount their horses and get ready to ride out and attack.

As the Kushite warriors step back to ram the gate once again, the gate flies open and the rest of the Delta fighters comes charging out.

The Delta fighters are led by Beirut, Kalili, Kwame, Rah, and two of the landing commanders they all charge out to give the Kushites hell.

Alsi, Jaugen, and Srtife are still holding their own, slewing everything in their way. Alsi then comes across Chief Zomi's and the Kuru village General Clay, who starts giving Alsi hell. Alsi is trying his best, but it seems all his best could do is keep him alive.

Srtife back is turned busy fighting, and is not aware of any of this.

Jaugen sees Alsi struggling, and runs over to help, but have no affect on General Clay.

General Clay simply dodges Jaugen's attacks, and knocks Jaugen down, then continues to attack Alsi. Just as General Clay is about to deliver the fatal blow to Alsi, out of nowhere comes Ben, who drives his sword through General Clay killing him.

Alsi and Jaugen are surprised to see General Clay die, but even more surprised when they notice that it was Ben who killed him. After killing General Clay, Ben walks over, and helps Alsi up onto his feet. Alsi is surprised to see Ben.

> ALSI
> Cousin I have never been more grateful to
> see you.

> BEN
> Save your flattering for later, there will be
> enough time to thank me after the war.

> JAUGEN
> What are you still doing here in the Delta?
> I thought you were tucked away safely in
> Kurgus by now.

> BEN
> I should have been. But the fight for the
> Delta is here in the Delta.

They all nod happy to see each other, then carry on fighting, covering each other's back.

Meanwhile Djer finally comes across Chief Bobo's and the Meroe village General Saku, and tells him that the Mumons are traitors, and they have injured Chief Bobo.

> DJER
> (to General Saku)
> General Saku, General Saku, Chief Bobo
> has been seriously injured.

> GENERAL SAKU
> Say what. Are you sure?

                    DJER
        Yes I am sure. He was just shot with an
        arrow, by a Mumon warrior. The Mumon
        warriors are here to betray the Empire.

                  GENERAL SAKU
        Where is the Chief now?

                    DJER
        Tifa is with him, just south of the
        compound gate.

General Saku immediately starts heading to go see if Chief Bobo is alright, when
from behind a Mumon traitor tries to stab him. Saku jumps out of the way, and they
begin fighting.

Meanwhile, Narmer is still killing everything in his way when he comes across Sting
and they square off.

Sting is on his horse when he spots Narmer. Sting charges at Narmer with his sword
cocked, screaming ready to chop Narmer's head off. But Narmer sees Sting coming,
and picks up a spear, and knocks Sting from his horse.

Sting gets up with his sword still in hand prepared for the show down.

                    STING
        I have been anticipating this moment for a
        while now. Eagerly waiting for the
        opportunity to see if you deserve the
        respect you demand. I personally think
        you are all talk.

                  CHIEF NARMER
        I am all talk. Ironically that seems to be all
        that you are doing right now. Come and
        please your-self, but be sure to come with
        more than that child's play attack, you
        just attempted. Because my combat skills
        grants me my respect!

They walk towards each other and the two starts battling with swords. They both
show incredible skills, but Narmer has the upper hand, convincingly having the
lesser struggle.

Sting gets careless, and Narmer gives him a cut. Sting pauses and gets upset, then charges at Narmer more aggressively. Narmer blocks everything effortlessly, and gives Sting another cut toying with him.

Sting gets even more upset and starts charging even harder, but once again Narmer blocks everything easily, and slices Sting stomach as Narmer ducks under one of Sting's wild swings.

Narmer then turns around to finish Sting, who is on one knee clutching his stomach, when Narmer spots an arrow coming straight at him, so he blocks it.

Narmer gets distracted, turns for a moment to see who the arrow came from, and Sting realizes the opportunity and slices Narmer across the chest.

Narmer staggers back and notices it was one of Prince Chala's warriors who tried to kill him. The traitor sends another shot at Narmer, at the same time Sting charges Narmer once again.

Narmer dodges the arrow and starts blocking the swings from Sting. Chala's traitor starts letting arrows fly rapidly, forcing Narmer to dodge constantly, which gives Sting the upper hand.

Sting begins to swing more aggressively, knocking Narmer off balance. Then out of nowhere appears Djer, who shoots the traitor in the chest with an arrow.

Narmer notices, feels relieved then together Djer and Narmer easily kills Sting. Djer then tells his father that Prince Chala's warriors are not the only traitors.

                         DJER
                    (to his father)
          There are a lot of traitors amongst us, the
          Mumons are also here to betray the
          Empire.

                    CHIEF NARMER
          The Mumon warriors and Prince Chala's
          warriors are working with the Delta. So
          then let them suffer the same faith, as the
          Foreigners of the Delta. Continue to
          spread the word to the Empire's loyal
          warriors.

                         DJER
          Yes Father.

Narmer and Djer nods to each other then go their separate ways, battling their enemies.

Duba and Fusa are still battling all the Delta Fighters that are charging out of the compound gate, when they come across the two landing commanders and they square off.

The commanders put up a good fight, but Duba and Fusa quickly kills them both. Duba and Fusa continue on slewing every Foreigner in their way.

They then come across Kwame and Rah, who put up a better fight, but they are also killed by Duba and Fusa. Duba and Fusa continue fighting on.

Tifa is still by Chief Bobo's side fighting, when Chief Bobo's General Saku runs over and kill the man Tifa is fighting, then asks Tifa for Bobo.

                    GENERAL SAKU
                     (to Tifa)
                Where is Chief Bobo?

Tifa points to Chief Bobo lying to the side looking dead.

General Saku runs over to Chief Bobo, kneels down next to Bobo and realizes Bobo is barely breathing.

General Saku holds Chief Bobo's head in his arms.

                    GENERAL SAKU
                My brother are you o.k.

                        BOBO
                  (choking on blood)
            No, not at all my brother. The Mumons.
            The Mumons. They are traitors. They did
            this to me.

                    GENERAL SAKU
                I know, I know, relax.

                        BOBO
            This seems like it could be where I make
            my transition.

General Saku looks at Bobo's wound.

GENERAL SAKU
Relax I will see to it that you are al-right.
And make sure whoever is responsible for
this, pays with their life. Every last one of
them!
(to Tifa)
Go and warn the rest of the Empire's
warriors.

Tifa takes off to go and do so. General Saku sits Bobo up respectfully and places his bow and arrows in his hand. Saku charges back into battle to do more killing.

Saku comes across one of the landing commanders, and kills him easily, and keeps moving through the battleground.

Bobo is on his last breath, and is still shooting arrows at the enemies.

Beirut and Kalili are still holding their own fighting, when Kalili comes across Zomi who has just finished killing a landing commander.

The two square off and they are very evenly matched at first, with both of them giving each other a couple cuts. But Kalili wins, simply by just being the better fighter. Kalili kills Zomi with no outside help.

Mnfeco is fighting a landing commander, and from a distance a Mumon traitor is taking aim at Mnfeco and is about to fire.

Tifa is coming, and spots the Mumon traitor about to shoot Mnfeco. Tifa runs and dive pulling Mnfeco out of the way of the arrow. Mnfeco realizes what just happened, and rises up sending a shot straight through the Mumon traitor's chest.

Mnfeco and Tifa then turns around and together they kill the landing commander.

MNFECO
(to Tifa)
I for one am now definitely grateful you
have joined us on this campaign. Thank
you for saving my life.

TIFA
A thanks from Chief Mnfeco, I need a
Witness to verify this moment.

208

                    MNFECO
          I see my praises flatter you. When this
          battle is over, I must find some way to
          repay you.

                     TIFA
          I will hold you to your words. But as of
          now we must stay focus, help me to
          spread the word that the Mumons are
          traitors.

                    MNFECO
          Will do, Warrior Princess.

Tifa and Mnfeco then go their separate ways to warn the rest of the Kushite
warriors.

Narmer is still killing everything in his way looking for traitors, when he spots Fusa
not too far away killing a landing commander. Narmer goes over to Fusa.

                  CHIEF NARMER
          The Mumon warriors, and Prince Chala
          warriors, are fighting for the Delta. The
          only reason they are here is to betray the
          Empire.

                     FUSA
          Are you certain?

                  CHIEF NARMER
          Yes I am certain. They have been trying to
          kill me.

As Narmer is trying to inform Fusa, an arrow comes flying at them. Narmer blocks it.
They both look over to see who it came from. It's one of Prince Chala's men.

The traitor realizes that Narmer and Fusa have spotted him, and he takes off
running. Narmer and Fusa take off after the traitor. They chase him for a little while.
Fusa sees the opportunity, cuts him off, and shoots him in the leg with an arrow
bringing him down.

The traitor starts crawling, knowing that Fusa is still coming. The traitor roles over
and tries to get a shot off, but Fusa notice and shoot the traitor in the arm disabling
him. Both Fusa and Narmer walk over to the traitor, and starts torturing him to talk.

Fusa stabs him in the leg with a sword.

FUSA
Who told you to kill Chief Narmer.

CHALA TRAITOR
(screams in pain)
Ahhhhh. Please, please. It was Prince
Chala. Please, I beg of you to spear my life.

FUSA
I am not the one you should be begging.

Narmer drives his spear through his heart.

CHIEF NARMER
It seems that Prince Chala is willing to go
to any extent to secure the crown. Well let
us see if he is capable of defeating the first
choice. Continue to warn the rest of the
Empire's warriors.

Fusa and Narmer knock spears together showing camaraderie, and then they split
up once again to go take care of the traitors, and the foreign invaders.

Ben, Jaugen, Alsi, Srtife plus a landing commander are in heavy combat against the
Kushites, Djer included.

Alsi begins to tell the other three to pull back, because he notices it's getting too
hectic. As they begin to move back, Djer sends a shot straight for Srtife who does not
see it coming.

Alsi sees it coming and jumps in front of the arrow, letting it hit him in the back,
instead of letting it hit his son Srtife. Srtife turns around, and find his father in his
face, trying not to show any signs of injury.

ALSI
(to Srtife)
Why have you stopped fighting, have you
forgotten that we are in the middle of a war.

SRTIFE
Father, are you okay?

ALSI
Never mind me, I am fine. Just keep
fighting.

Srtife looks over his father's shoulder to see who shot the arrow, and spots Djer. Srtife charges Djer enraged, as Alsi tries to hold him back, but it's too late, Srtife is in Djer's face swinging wildly. Alsi tries to go help Srtife, but Jaugen and Ben hold him back.

ALSI
Son noooooo. We must stay together.

Srtife charges over to Djer.

JAUGEN
(holds Alsi back)
Alsi noooo. We must fall back and take cover.

ALSI
(tries to pull away)
I must go and help Srtife.

JAUGEN
Srtife is a-lright. He will catch up. We
must get you out of harm's way.

Ben and Jaugen takes Alsi off to the side, as Djer and Srtife, continue to fight on. Srtife is sloppy in the beginning, because he is fighting with too much anger, which gives Djer the upper hand.

SRTIFE
(swings wildly)
I will kill the bloody lot of you Kushites.

DJER
(blocks easily)
Well then you have got to get your skills
up beyond that of an apprentice.

Srtife gets angrier and comes harder. Djer and Srtife battle on for a while, with Srtife holding his own, but never getting the upper hand.

Djer gives Srtife a couple slices then knocks the sword out of Srtife's hand and trips him. Djer stands over Srtife to finish him, when out of nowhere an arrow hits Djer in the chest.

It came from the Mumon traitor that has been chasing him. Srtife sees that Djer have been hit, so Srtife kicks Djer back and roles over onto his feet and pick up his sword. Srtife once again charges Djer but now has the upper hand, because of Djer's injury.

Djer tries his best to defend himself, but the injury plus Srtife proves to be too much. Djer gets overwhelmed and as a result Srtife kills Djer.

After killing Djer, Srtife tries to look for Ben and Jaugen with his father, but Srtife does not see them anywhere.

Then suddenly, another warrior attacks Srtife, forcing him to defend himself. In the midst of all the confusion Srtife loses track of his father them all together.

Duba is still killing everything in his way, when he comes across Beirut, who is killing everything in his way. The two spots each other and they square off.

> DUBA
> Beirut it seems my dreams have finally
> come true. I have spent sleepless nights
> thinking about killing you.

> BEIRUT
> I 'm proud to know that I have been giving
> you nightmares.

> DUBA
> Nightmare, not in this lifetime. It was
> definitely a deja 'vu, a deja 'vu of me
> separating your head from your body.

Duba charges in swinging at Beirut, and they square off, first with spears. They both show their extraordinary skills, both holding their own. But Duba seems to have the upper hand, piercing Beirut here and there. They battle on until Duba knocks the spear out of Beirut's hand.

Duba charges in to finish Beirut, but Beirut pulls out his sword and chops Duba's spear in half as Duba charges.

Duba pauses to look at his spear in half, then drops it, and pulls out his sword, and the two starts battling again.

Again they battle on for a while, with Duba still having the upper hand, Duba gives Beirut a couple slices as they go along.

Then out of nowhere, Duba gets hit in the back with an arrow. Duba falls to one knee, and Beirut turns to see who shot Duba. It was the Mumon's General Masa, and when Masa shot the arrow, Fusa spotted him and heads after Masa.

Beirut turns back around to continue fighting Duba. Beirut now sees his opportunity that Duba is injured, and charges Duba while Duba is still down, and proceed to try and chop Duba's head off.

Duba starts blocking, but now is having a hard time because of his injury. Never the less, Duba battles on. Only now with Beirut gaining the upper hand.

Fusa catches up to the Mumon's General Masa and confronts him. Fusa jumps off his horse and they square off.

FUSA
(jumps off his horse)
Masa you worthless traitor, you and the
Mumon warriors would dare betray your
brothers of the Empire.

GENERAL MASA
There is no brother hood amongst us.
Only paradise if those in power smile
upon you. And let us be honest, the
Empire stopped smiling at the Mumon
village a long time ago.

FUSA
I could assure you I for one am no longer
smiling. And I promise you when this
battle is done every Momon woman will be
a widow, and every child a bastard.

Fusa and Masa charge each other and begin battling with spears. They fight for a while both putting up a good fight.

They continue on fighting, with neither seeming to have the upper hand, both blocking each other's attack. When all of a sudden General Masa makes a mistake and Fusa delivers the fatal blow.

Fusa then pulls out his spear, and in a rush mounts his horse, and heads over to go help Duba.

Duba and Beirut are still fighting, and Beirut still has the upper hand due to Duba's injury. Duba is still putting up a good fight, but Beirut is proving to be too much for Duba. Beirut gets Duba down and is about to deliver the deathblow, when Fusa comes charging towards them on his horse.

Fusa throw his spear straight through Beirut killing him. As he is dying Beirut drives his sword through Duba, killing him.

Beirut then falls on top of Duba. Both Beirut and Duba dies, as Fusa gets to them only to realize that he is too late. Fusa pulls his spear out of Beirut, and in anger stabs Beirut's dead body a couple more times.

Fusa then kneels down by Duba in respect, and closes Duba's eyes. Fusa then snaps back into war mode. Fusa gets up enraged, and starts killing every enemy in his way.

Meanwhile Mnfeco is fighting a Mumon traitor. Mnfeco kills the traitor then crosses path with Kalili. Mnfeco get excited, because he has wanted this opportunity for awhile.

                    MNFECO
              (to Kalili, vigorously)
          Finally the ancestors have answered my
          prayers. So long have I yearned for the
          day, that I would get the chance to open
          your chest, to see if you have a heart.

                    KALILI

          You know what they say, be careful what
          you wish for. But if it is all the same, I will
          save you the trouble and answer your
          question for you. No, I have no heart.

                    MNFECO
          Even though I myself have came to that
          same conclusion. I know that's
          impossible, so I must verify it for myself,
          and get physical proof.

Mnfeco rushes Kalili and they square off. They start fighting, and continue on for a while.

Ben, Jaugen, and Alsi are still fighting. They are in the midst of it all, fighting individual men holding their own, but Alsi is under pressure because of his injury.

The warrior Alsi is fighting cuts him again and again making Alsi even weaker. Ben realizes what is going on, and quickly kills the man he is fighting, and rushes over to help Alsi.

Ben attacks the warrior Alsi is fighting, and kills him also. Ben then goes to check on Alsi to see if he is alright.

BEN
Are you alright?

ALSI
(kneels in agony)
I 'm alright. LOOK OUT.

The Hierak village General Ourou comes from Ben's blind side, and tries to chop his head off. Ben blocks it, roles onto his feet, and they start battling. They battle for a while, but General Ourou has the obvious upper hand, he has Ben struggling not to be killed.

Alsi realizes what is going on, and gets up to help Ben. They start double teaming General Ourou. But General Ourou even though under pressure, is holds his own, dancing around both Alsi and Ben, slicing them here and there.

All of a sudden General Ourou knocks the sword out of Alsi's hand and picks it up. Ben in attempt to stop Ourou charges General Ourou more aggressively, but gets a serious cut, and loses his sword.

General Ourou puts his sword to Ben's neck, and is about to slice it, when Alsi in desperation throws his body at General Ourou. General Ourou tries to shield Alsi off, but Alsi still lands at Ourou's feet, and locks on preventing Ourou from being able to move.

General Ourou starts stabbing Alsi in the back trying to get lose.

BEN
(screams)
NOOOOOOO

Ben in anger picks back up his sword and stabs General Ourou, killing him. General Ourou falls to his death.

Ben then kneels down, and roles Alsi over to check on him.

BEN
Oh cousin, I am so sorry this happened to you.

ALSI
(choking on blood)
Everything will be al-right my cousin. I have no regrets

BEN
Relax do not talk. I will take care of you.

ALSI
Cousin, I, I beg of you, please look after
my son Srtife.

Alsi's eyes close, as he dies in Ben's arms. Ben pauses for a moment.

Jaugen runs over, and is shocked when he sees what has happened. Jaugen pauses
for a moment, then comes back to reality.

JAUGEN
Let's go my friend, we must keep moving.

BEN
We cannot just leave him here like this.

JAUGEN
We must. He is dead. And we are still in
the middle of a war.

Ben know Jaugen is right and lay Alsi's dead body down. Ben composes himself and
they move on.

Mnfeco and Kalili are in the middle of their battle. Kalili is doing al-right holding his
own. Kalili is an excellent fighter giving Mnfeco a few cuts here and there. Never the
less, the monstrous Mnfeco proves to be too much for Kalili to handle. Mnfeco toys
with Kalili humiliating him, then kills him.

Meanwhile Narmer is fighting two of the landing commanders, while trying to stay
on alert for traitors. When in the middle of fighting Narmer notices an arrow coming
towards him, and he blocks it. Narmer turns to see who the arrow came from, and it
was Prince Chala.

The two landing commanders keep attacking, forcing Narmer to pay attention. And
as they do so, Prince Chala starts letting arrows fly on rapid, one after the other.

Narmer is on the defense dodging arrows, and blocking the fighters at the same
time. Then Narmer pushes one of the commanders into an arrow killing him.

Narmer then continues to fight the other commander, while still dodging arrows.
They go on for a while then Narmer kills the second landing commander, and
charges after Prince Chala who is still shooting arrows at him.

Narmer gets closer by having to block and dodge arrows. When Narmer gets In close, he blocks an arrow with his shield, but the arrow goes through the shield, and pierces Narmer forearm.

Still Narmer gets to Chala not missing a step. He gets in Chala's face, sword swinging, trying to chop Prince Chala's head off.

Ben and Jaugen are still fighting trying to stay alive as they go along. They are both fighting separate warriors when the injured Ben comes across Chief Bobo's Meroe village General Saku, and they square off.

General Saku with all his anger after seeing Chief Bobo injured still boiling inside of him, takes easy advantage of Ben. The injured Ben puts up a good fight, but is no match for a healthy Saku. Saku easily over powers Ben and kills him and moves on.

It happened so quickly, that Jaugen didn't even see it happen because he was too busy fighting with his back turned. After Ben receives his deathblow, he staggers off, and dies propped up against a wall. Which left him looking as if he is still alive and still standing. Jaugen finish killing his man, and turns around looking for Ben. Jaugen notices Ben standing up against a wall, and goes over to call him.

When Jaugen gets over there, he calls Ben's name, and touches Ben on the shoulder. Ben's dead body falls back into Jaugen's arms. Jaugen is shocked, and lays Ben's dead body down. He pauses for a moment to collect him-self.

Jaugen does so, then comes to his senses, and continue moving, trying to protect his life. The war is still going on strong but some of the Delta fighters are beginning to surrender.

Meanwhile Narmer and Prince Chala are in the middle of their fight, using spears. Even though Narmer is injured, he is still getting the best of Prince Chala. The Prince is putting up a good fight, just as aggressive every step of the way.

Some of the Kushite warriors begin circling around, to observe the fight. Narmer is still maintaining the upper hand, when out of nowhere Prince Chala's General Hara ups, and shoots an arrow hitting Narmer. Before Hara could get another shot off, Fusa shoots him from across the way, and General Hara's own unit next to him begins to stab General Hara, attacking him and killing him.

All the Kushite warriors look on in an up roar, while Fusa has an arrow cocked looking for any other traitors. Prince Chala charges Narmer and tries to take advantage while Narmer is injured. Prince Chala begins swinging aggressively, sending Narmer back blocking. The Prince then pauses to grin, and taunt Narmer.

PRINCE CHALA
Is this the best you could do to help
yourself. You are pathetic, and King Salo
thinks you are worthy of wearing my
crown.

CHIEF NARMER
So this is what we 're doing now? You
have betrayed your Empire just to wear
the crown. What would ever make you
think the people you have turned your
back on, would want you as the King of
their Empire.

PRINCE CHALA
But that's where you 're wrong Narmer. I
haven't betrayed my Empire. I 'm just
securing what's rightfully mine, while
making it obviously clear that you aren't
worthy, to be mentioned amongst our
lineage of Kings of the Kushite Empire.

CHIEF NARMER
You are not man enough to complete such
a task.

Narmer gets reenergize and breaks the arrow in his shoulder. Narmer then charges
the Prince swinging, trying to knock his head off.

The Prince tries to defend himself but it makes no difference, because Narmer is
now upset, and Earth has no force that could match Narmer's furry when he is
angry. The Prince last a little while, but Narmer's determination is too much for him.

Narmer drives his sword in the Prince's stomach killing him. The warriors of the
Empire cheers, as if they had just won the battle. Narmer pulls his sword out of
Prince Chala, and stabs him again, then falls to one knee exhausted in pain. Fusa, and
Mnfeco rushes over to Narmer, and helps him up.

MNFECO
Are you okay my brother?

CHIEF NARMER
I will be fine.

The crowd sees Narmer stand to his feet and cheers even louder. Fusa and Mnfeco help Narmer off to the side. The Kushite warriors carry on fighting with a new burst of energy as if they 're winning for Narmer.

Some of the Delta fighters are now fleeing from the Kushites. Some are surrendering. While others are still putting up a fight those who are still fighting, are getting killed by the Kushite warriors.

Fusa ties a cloth around Narmer's wound to stop the bleeding. Chief Rasa runs over to inform Narmer.

                    GENERAL RASA
          Some foreign fighters are fleeing north
          towards the sea, possibly to try and
          escape by boat.

                    CHIEF NARMER
          I want no foreign invader to get away.
          They were eager to come to our land, and
          I am just as eager to issue out there
          judgment.
                    (to Fusa and Mnfeco)
          General Fusa round up a unit on
          horseback, so that we could go and fetch
          the fleeing fighters before they escape by
          sea. Chief Mnfeco I want you and Chief
          Rasa with the remaining warriors, to
          finish rounding up the foreign fighters
          that are surrendering, and continue
          killing the ones that have not.

They all nod in agreement, then walks off to go do their duty. Narmer then walks over to his drummer, flag holder, sandal bearer, messenger, and horse keeper. Narmer mounts his horse.

                    CHIEF NARMER
                    (to Messenger)
          Go and notify our reinforcement at Buba.
          Tell them to come forth. Victory is ours.

                    MESSENGER
          Yes, right away Chief Narmer.

The messenger mounts a horse and rides off.

Narmer then rides over to Fusa who is lined up with other warriors on horseback, yelling warrior cries. Narmer and posse then ride out to go stop the fleeing foreign fighters. They ride for a while, then starts catching up to fleeing foreign fighters on foot and then some on horseback.

Whenever and wherever the Kushite warriors catch the fleeing foreign fighters, who are terrified and running for their lives. The Kushites kill them like a predator killing its prey. The Kushites warriors kill as they go along with no mercy.

As the Kushites get closer to the Mediterranean Sea they notice that some of the foreign fighters have already made it onto boats, and are trying to sail away. Narmer, Fusa, and the other warriors charge towards the shoreline, and starts shooting fire arrows at the boats.

The foreign fighters shoots arrows back at the warriors on shore. But eventually the fire arrows get the best of the foreign fighters, and catch their boats afire. The fighters on the boats are forced to abandon ship before it is too late. The fighters all jump off the boats as the boats burn and sink. Fusa, Narmer, and all the warriors on shore starts cheering, when they see the last boat sink.

The Kushite warriors begin rejoicing, and mocking the foreign fighters as they drown at sea. The Kushite warriors round up the surviving exhausted foreign fighters as they swim back to the shore.

Narmer and Fusa look at each other satisfied, then turn their horses around, and ride back to Sais. Narmer and Fusa get back to Sais, and the majority of the fighting has stopped. Except for the Kushite warriors rounding up the Delta fighters, and having to kill the ones who are still resisting every now and then.

Narmer and Fusa, see Mnfeco across the way talking to the King, and rides over to addresses the King. Both Narmer and Fusa ride over, gets off their horses, and kneel in respect to greet the King.

CHIEF NARMER
(kneels)
Greetings my King. The Empire's warriors
honor your presence.

KING SALO
Narmer my son, please stand up. All
praises are due onto you and the Empire's
warriors. I should be on my knees
honoring you, General Fusa, and the rest
of the Empire's warriors.

                    CHIEF NARMER
You are too gracious my King. Your
contributions towards this war campaign
was just as important as anyone else's in
the Empire.

                    KING SALO
Congratulations to you on leading a
successful war, against the Delta.

They walk together.

                    CHIEF NARMER
Thank you my King. We were successful
because of the warriors of the Empire.
Many of whom were more anxious to be
here, than myself. With such loyalty it is
impossible for any adversary to defeat
this Empire.

                    KING SALO
You see such loyalty because the people
of this Empire believe in you. You feel
their pain and because of that they will
face any enemy with you.
                    (beat)
Chief Mnfeco told me of the betrayal by
Prince Chala and the Mumon warriors.

                    CHIEF NARMER
Yes, They were both here to betray the
Empire. Them and others in there-

                    KING SALO
No explanation is necessary. Prince Chala
knew when this war was over, so was any
opportunity of him being successor. And
as for the Mumons, let us not forget this
was a war, and this is precisely what
happens in a war. Your enemies will
reveal them-selves. All that is important is
that you, and the Empire's warriors have
prevailed against the foreign invaders.
Everything else-

GENERAL SAKU
Greetings King Salo, Chief Narmer. Pardon
me for interrupting, but Chief Narmer
there is something that you must see.

CHIEF NARMER
What is it?

GENERAL SAKU
It's Djer.

Chief Narmer runs off to go see. Narmer pushes his way through the crowd, and gets
to the center, only to see Djer's lifeless body lying on the ground. Narmer is
devastated. Falls to his knees, lift Djer's lifeless body in his arms, and lets out aloud
cry.

CHIEF NARMER
(screams)
NOOOOOOOOOO.
(talks to himself)
My first-born son. How could this be? How
could your life be over, when your future
looks so promising? Almighty Ntchru I ask
you why.

FUSA
(kneels beside Narmer)
I too mourn the loss of Djer, but now is
not the time to mourn. You must be
strong cousin. The eyes of the Empire are
watching you.

CHIEF NARMER
(upset)
Is it wrong to mourn my own son.

Fusa puts his hand on his shoulder.

FUSA
Cousin that could never be wrong. But at
this moment you are the leader of the
warriors of the Kushite Empire, and you
have just led us to victory in a war. We all
look to you as a source of strength, this is
not the time to break, or show weakness.

Narmer looks up at Fusa knowing he is right. He holds Djer's lifeless body close to him, in attempt to give Djer one final hug.

Suddenly Narmer notices on the arrow sticking out of Djer's chest is the Mumon's trademark. Narmer lays Djer's dead body down, then pulls out the arrow, and begins staring at it.

Fusa notices Narmer staring at the Mumon's trademark and knows exactly what Narmer is thinking.

                    CHIEF NARMER
          I want every Mumon here gathered, and
          lined up in front of me at once.

                    FUSA
          Now you 're speaking and reacting as a
          leader.

Fusa eagerly starts doing as Narmer asked.

                    MNFECO
          My brother what do you have in mind?

Chief Narmer stands and does not answer.

                    CHIEF NARMER
                    (shouts)
          I want every Mumon here, rounded up,
          and in front of me at once. And if any of
          them should try to resist, do not hesitate
          to kill them. That is only confirmation that
          they are traitors of our Kushite Empire.

The Kushite warriors begin to do as Narmer ordered, but they are all looking puzzled. The warriors start removing the Mumons from amongst the foreign prisoners.

Jaugen and Srtife are amongst the foreign prisoners.

Some Mumons are also being taken from amongst the Kushite warriors some that were not even being held as prisoners.

Mnfeco tries to reason with Narmer.

MNFECO

I know revenge seems soothing at the
moment, but that will not change anything.

CHIEF NARMER
(oddly calm)
I have already grasped that reality. I am
just going to make sure I send who ever
took Djer's life, to join him.

MNFECO
(pleads)
And what would that change.

CHIEF NARMER

The Empire will have one less traitor.
Line up the Madjai marks men.

MNFECO

Chief Narmer, I ask you to please reconsider.

CHIEF NARMER
(loudly)
And I am asking you Chief Mnfeco to line
up the Madjai marks men. Just line up any
of the Empire's warriors, is that too much
to ask.

MNFECO

Right away. I will see to it.

Mnfeco walks away to go do as Narmer asked. King Salo walks over to console
Narmer, and to tries and reason with him.

KING SALO

Chief Narmer I empathize with you, and
know exactly how you are feeling right
now. For I too have lost sons in the past.
And I know there is nothing you could do
to fill that void, revenge may seem like
soothing sweet retribution and justice,
but it will not bring Djer back.

CHIEF NARMER
Then let my revenge be a soothing void.
For they have already taken one of my
joys of this reality.

KING SALO
But this was a war young ruler.
Unfortunately this was a war, and in a
war there will always be unfortunate
circumstances that one must accept.

CHIEF NARMER
And I will accept nothing less than every
last one of these traitors paying with their
lives.

The King sees that Narmer wont be persuaded, so he nods and says no more.
Narmer pauses and takes another look at Djer's dead body.

CHIEF NARMER
Please my King, I ask of you to please have
Djer's body transported back to Nekheb.

KING SALO
Certainly young ruler, I will have it taken
care of right away.

CHIEF NARMER
Thank you, my King.

Narmer looks at Djer's body one last time, and walks away in anger. All of the
Mumon warriors are lined up and bound together. They are all pleading for their
lives, claiming they had nothing to do with the betrayal. Fusa and the Madjai marks
men are lined up across from the Mumons waiting on their orders. Narmer still
angry mounts his horse, and starts riding towards Fusa and the Madjai marks men.
Fusa rides out to meet Narmer halfway.

CHIEF NARMER
(to Fusa)
If any of the Mumons should try and flee.
Have the Madjai marks men kill them.

FUSA
It will be an honor and my pleasure.

They part ways, and Narmer rides over to the Mumon prisoners. And with everyone to bear witness the King, Chiefs, Generals, warriors, and captured foreign fighters all looking. Narmer gets off his horse.

                    CHIEF NARMER
          My son Djer was killed by this arrow.
          Which bear the Mumon's trademark,
          because of that one fact, I will kill every
          Mumon here.

Everyone GASPS.

                    CHIEF NARMER
          Then I will go to the Mumon village, and
          kill every Mumon man there, because you
          all are probably infected with this sick
          Gene to betray our Empire.

A loud continuous plea and cry continues to come from the Mumon prisoners, but their cries fall on deaf ears.

Narmer just pulls out his sword and begins killing all of the Mumon prisoners. Some try to escape when they realize that Narmer will not spear them, so they instead gets killed by the Madjai marks men as they try to flee.

The others stand and beg declaring their innocence, but only to meet the wrath of Narmer's sword.

The foreign prisoners are all scared and worried, as they witness Narmer's fury.

                    JAUGEN
          (to Srtife)
          These Kushites will never change. They
          have just won a war, and already they are
          killing each other.

                    SRTIFE
          (upset)
          Who cares if they are killing each other, at
          least more of those bastards will be dead.

Narmer goes on killing, in his mad man's rage. Narmer kills all the Mumon prisoners by himself, except for those who tried to escape.

He kills all day long. He kills until it starts to turn to night. Covered in blood, Narmer refuses to stop.

The other warriors, looks on thinking Narmer has gone mad, so they all have given up on trying to reason with him.

The Mumon prisoners are still begging for their lives, but still Narmer shows them no mercy.

Narmer goes on killing well into the night. He then gets to the last Mumon prisoner and pushes his sword through his stomach. Covered in blood Narmer pauses to gaze back at all of the Mumon's dead bodies.

Mnfeco, and the King have been watching Narmer the entire time, thinking he has lost his mind. Narmer then walks over to Fusa and says.

> CHIEF NARMER
> Prepare the Nekheb warriors, and be
> ready to ride. We leave for the Mumon
> village at first light.

> KING SALO
> Young ruler surely that was enough lives
> taken, to vindicate the Mumons of their
> betrayal.

> CHIEF NARMER
> There could never be enough lives taken,
> if it is for my flesh and blood.
>   (beat)
> If it is for the ones I love. And in case you
> have forgotten, because of the Mumon's
> betrayal Chief Duba is dead. Chief Bobo is
> dead. Mnfeco's General Ourou is dead.
> Rasa's General Bungo is dead. They are all
> dead, and you think the lives of these few
> worthless traitors, should vindicate the
> Mumon village for the lives of so many of
> our enlighten leaders.

> KING SALO
> I am aware of all our prominent leaders
> that have been killed. It was I whom
> painfully had to send their dead bodies
> back to their respected villages in honor.
> And killing every Mumon will not change
> that fact.
>   (beat)

Yes you are Djer's father which makes
your love stronger, but we all loved Djer,
he will be missed by the entire Empire.
The same for every member of this
Empire, that was lost during this battle.
But I must state once again, this was a
war young ruler, wars are unpredictable,
and unforgiving. And we must accept that.

CHIEF NARMER
Wars are unpredictable and unforgiving.
Yes that I will accept, but a traitor to my
Empire, that I will not.
(to Fusa)
As I have said, prepare the Nekheb
warriors to ride at first light.

FUSA
Yes my Chief, we will be ready.

Narmer nods seriously, and they all nod back. Narmer turns and walks away.

Time passes and the Sun light begins to break the darkness of the night, and the
Nekheb warriors are all lined up and ready to ride.

Narmer and Fusa are at the head of the posse. Narmer gives the signal, and the
warriors all ride out following him.

The King, Mnfeco, Tifa, and all the remaining warriors watch them leave. Narmer
and posse heads out on their journey, and this time Narmer is looking more
determined and vicious than ever.

They get to the Nile, and they get onto awaiting boats and head south to the Mumon
village.

They get there, dock their boats, and ride ashore. Narmer and posse starts riding
through the town, which looks a little better, but there is still a lot of damage from
the Aswan and Mumon war.

The Mumon community sees Narmer, and his Nekheb warriors coming, and quickly
gets out of their way. Narmer and warriors rides straight to Jusa's residence. When
Narmer and posse get there, a young warrior comes out to greet them, by kneeling
before Narmer.

PEN
(kneels)
Greetings Chief Narmer, praises be to
your name. We humbly honor your visit.

Chief Narmer gets off his horse.

CHIEF NARMER
Where is Jusa.

PEN
We the Mumon people are currently
holding him as prisoner inside his home.

CHIEF NARMER
Your Chief is being held captive in his
own home. What on earth is going on up
here with the Mumon people?

PEN
My apologies Chief Narmer, for any
confusion the Mumon village might have
caused. Honestly speaking until you just
arrived, we ourselves were confused
about what is actually going on in our
own village.

CHIEF NARMER
Go on.

PEN
Ever since the meeting of the council, we
were all told by Chief Jusa, that we wouldn't
be taking part in any campaign against the
Delta. Then three weeks ago Beirut of Sais
visited our village, and three days ago there
was a substantial size gift delivered here to
Chief Jusa from Beirut and the Delta
residents. We later found out after taking
Jusa prisoner, that the gift was five hundred
thousand pounds of gold. Then upon
delivery of the gift from Beirut and the
Delta residents, General Masa started
selecting a chosen few Mumon warriors.
Then two days ago the General and those
chosen few, left saying that they were going

to assist in the war. This is the point at
which we became convinced, because
countless others including myself
volunteered to go, but General Masa denied
us, saying that our support was not needed.
And now you showing up here in these
times, in such numbers, only confirms what
we the Mumon people has suspected all
along. Chief Jusa sent General Masa to aid
the Delta, and betray the Empire.

CHIEF NARMER
And how is the Empire to know, that all
the Mumons people are not traitors?

PEN
The Empire should see our loyalty,
because we the Mumon people are in the
middle of overthrowing our Chief, whom
we the Mumon people only suspected of
betraying the Empire.

CHIEF NARMER
This could just be another chapter in the
treachery of the Mumon people. If the
Mumon people are not traitors of the
Empire as you claim. Bring the captured
Jusa out in front of me, and hand me his
head.

PEN
Right away Chief Narmer.

Pen the young warrior accompanied by two other warriors, walk inside and comes
out with Jusa tied up. Pen walks Jusa over in front of Narmer, and puts Jusa to kneel
down.

Jusa pleas and begs Narmer for help, saying that his village have wrongfully
imprisoned him. Jusa goes on begging, but Narmer just stares at him coldly with no
reply. The two warriors hold Jusa down, while Pen the young warrior steps forward,
and with one swing, chops Jusa's head off.

Pen the young warrior then picks up Jusa's severed head, and hands it to Narmer.
Narmer accepts it as a sign of loyalty, then holds Jusa's severed head in the air and
says.

CHIEF NARMER
(holds up servered head)
Let this severed head of the traitor Jusa, be
the cornerstone, which the new Mumon
leadership is built around.

PEN
(kneels)
So let it be, because the Mumon people
are loyal subjects of our Kushite Empire.
The actions of our late Chief Jusa in no
way represents the true values of us, the
Mumon people.

CHIEF NARMER
You may stand young warrior. What is
your name?

PEN
(stands proudly)
Honorable Chief. My name is Pen.

CHIEF NARMER
Pen I commend what you and the Mumon
people have done here. Your people have
gone through a lot recently, and are
looking at rougher days ahead. They will
need someone strong to lead them through
these times. There will be a celebration at
Nekheb to celebrate the Empires victory
over the Delta. You and the rest of the
Mumon people are all welcome.

Narmer and Pen shake hands and nod to each other once again in respect. Then
Narmer with Jusa's severed head still in hand, gets back on his horse. Narmer and
posse then turn and start riding out. The Mumon locals watch Narmer and posse
ride off into the distance. Narmer with Jusa's severed head still in his hand.

EXT. NEKHEB - DAY

Narmer and posse head home. They get to Nekheb, where the Empire is already
celebrating the victory. When the people of Nekheb see Narmer and the warriors
riding into town, they erupt and give them a hero's welcome.

Narmer and posse rides in and some of the warriors stop to celebrate with the people, but Narmer heads straight home going to see his family. Narmer walks into his house, and finds Berenib comforting the other children.

Narmer enters as his youngest son Kem is asking Berenib about Djer.

> KEM
> But mother why did this have to happen?

> BERENIB
> This is nothing unusual my son. Dying is a part of the process of life. This is something that we must all accept, for eventually all living thing will make the transition. And a battlefield is often where brave men, like your brother Djer often make their transition.

Chief Narmer's daughter FEEZZE sees her father walking up.

> FEEZZE
> Father! Father!

Feezze runs to Narmer, happy to see him, and gives him a big hug. The other children runs over, also screaming father. They hug Narmer as if they haven't seen him in years, despite the fact that Narmer is covered in blood. Narmer kneels down and give all his children one big hug.

> FEEZZE
> (hugs tightly)
> Oh father, I am so happy to see you.

Berenib stands up and sheds a tear. She is so happy to see Narmer.

> CHIEF NARMER
> I am happy to see you also, my love.
> (beat)
> I am relieved to see you all.

> FEEZZE
> (concerned)
> How are you father, were you injured?

> CHIEF NARMER
> No my dear daughter. I am fine.

                    KEM
              (ingenuously)
Father, have you heard of what has
happened to Djer?

              CHIEF NARMER
Yes, I have my son.

                    KEM
Mother said not to be sad. Because a
battlefield is where brave men like Djer
make their transition.

              CHIEF NARMER
Yes it is my son. And your brother Djer
was a brave man. That died for his people.
So be proud, and hold your heads high for
the honor of being able to call him your
brother.

                    KEM
I will father.

Narmer nods to Kem then stands up to greet Berenib. Narmer walks over to
Berenib, falls to his knees, and tightly hugs her around her waist.

Berenib hugs Narmer with tears still in her eyes overcome with emotions, so
relieved to see Narmer.

              BERENIB
              (hugs Narmer)
Welcome home my love. I am so relieved
to see you. I have yearned for your return
since the moment you left.

              CHIEF NARMER
Oh my love, I am so dreadfully sorry. For
my neglect have taken the life of our son.
Only if I had stayed with-

              BERENIB
My love this is not yours, or anyone else's
fault. The will of time could never be
accredited to no man.

CHIEF NARMER
But he is my son. I should have made it
my duty to keep him out of harms way. I
should have protected him.

BERENIB
My love I know you did all you could have.
Death is often the wages of war. So I beg
of you, do not let this tragedy burden you.
Come let me wash and clean the blood
from your body, and prepare ourselves to
attend the celebrations with the rest of
the Empire.

Berenib and Narmer look into each other's eyes, and stand up together. Finally
someone has gotten through to Narmer. Berenib begins to take off Narmer's armor.

The two walk off together to the bath. While Berenib and Narmer walk off to the
bath, their next oldest son SHAK starts staring at his father's spear, with Jusa's
severed head still on it.

Shak walks over and picks up the spear, to get a closer look. Shak is impressed, and
starts touching the severed head, he then walks out onto the balcony with the spear
in his hand. Shak stands, and gazes out at the village.

Narmer is in the bath with five wives bathing him. They all pamper Narmer like a
King, cleaning every inch of his body. His wives finish bathing him, then Narmer gets
out of the tub and his wives attend to his wounds. The wives put some medicine on
Narmer's wounds, and then bandage him up. They finish nursing Narmer. He then
begins getting ready.

Narmer is putting on his garments, when Berenib comes around the corner looking
beautiful. Berenib walks over, and helps Narmer with the last piece of his garments.

CHIEF NARMER
I only wish our son was here, to witness
this moment.

BERENIB
Djer is not here to witness it, but you do
have sons here to bear witness. Sons
whom think that you are the greatest
thing that ever walked this Earth. And
trust me. They will never forget this
moment for as long as they live.

Berenib and Narmer turns to look at their two sons Shak and Kem, still on the balcony, still holding the spear with Jusa's severed head, as they overlook the village. Berenib and Narmer stare at them felling proud, then turns and walk off together heading to the celebration.

They get outside and as soon as the crowd sees them, they erupt in cheering. The crowd starts chanting Narmer's name as Berenib and Narmer passes through.

CROWD
Narmer, Narmer, Narmer, Narmer.

Berenib and Narmer continue through the crowd, as the crowd continues to chant Narmer's name. They pass through the crowd and get to Nekheb hall where the King, Mnfeco, Fusa, and all the other Chiefs and Generals are on a balcony addressing the Empire's people, while waiting on Narmer to arrive.

Narmer and Berenib walks in, and when the leaders recognize them, they all start praising Narmer. Berenib stands to the side, and starts applauding Narmer also.

All the leaders of the Empire starts coming over one by one to kneel down before Narmer, and praise him. Even the King comes over, and bows before Narmer and praises him.

Narmer then walks out onto the balcony. As soon as the people of the Empire get a glimpse of Narmer they all erupt. They all start chanting again.

Srtife, Jaugen, and all the other foreign prisoners of the Delta, are now being held in Nekheb. Jaugen and the other prisoners hear the chants.

JAUGEN
This is the last thing that the foreign
population needs. The Empire is now
praising this maniac. Now he will surely
be crowned King.

SRTIFE
Who cares, who is King? We will still be
their prisoners.

JAUGEN
Who becomes King determines our
treatment as their prisoners. Which you
will come to see is not always such a bad
thing, if they decide to spare our lives.
Especially now that we are back in the
south inland! The south inland is where

235

the Empire have forbidden us to come freely for decades, and now we have lost a war and they bring us here willingly. Isn't that ironic, even in defeat there is a valuable lesson to be learn, and if learned you could fine your victory. That way your experience would not have been a total lost. But if Narmer becomes King, the chance of our lives being speared is almost impossible.

Narmer waves to the Empire's people. He gets them to be quiet, so that he could address them.

>   CHIEF NARMER
> People of the Kushite Empire, I am honored by the overwhelming welcome I have received since returning from the Delta. I am also honored to have fought alongside and for you, the most powerful Empire in the world, the Kushite Empire. So to you all I give my praises, every single one of you. It is truly an honor to be a member of this Empire. For today I can say we all stood together, and took back full control of your land. This is an accomplishment beyond measure, so to you all I say celebrate, and be filled with joy. For you all have earned it.

The crowd erupts with cheers. Narmer bows and keeps waving as they chant his name. Narmer then turns, and walks over to the King.

>   CHIEF NARMER
>   (to King Salo)
> King Salo, I have decided to accept your offer.

>   KING SALO
> And what offer would that be.

>   CHIEF NARMER
> The only offer that is relevant, you naming your successor.

                    KING SALO
Young Ruler, I have waited for years to
here you say those words.
                    (beat)
May I ask you, what made you change
your mind?

                    CHIEF NARMER
The Empire is at a cross road, and needs
someone to lead them in the right
direction, and its like you have always
said, if not me then who.

                    KING SALO
If not you, then nobody, because you are
our Empire's true leader.

They shake hands.

                    KING SALO
I will make the announcement, and I will
prepare the Empire for the crowning
ceremony. MY KING.

                    CHIEF NARMER
I have not been crowned as yet, so all
praises are still due onto you. MY KING.

                    KING SALO
Narmer I thank you for accepting this
duty, now I could truly live the rest of my
days a happy man.

                    CHIEF NARMER
And I thank you my King, for always
believing in me. You saw all of this for me,
even when I didn't see it for myself. I
thank you.

The King and Narmer nod to each other in respect. The King walks towards the
balcony to make the announcement.

Narmer walks over to talk to Berenib, Fusa, Mnfeco and all the other leaders. They
don't know what is going on as yet, they are paying attention to the King like
everyone else, when they hear the King making the announcement.

>   KING SALO
>   Loyal people of the Kushite Empire, I have
>   an announcement to make.
>   (beat)
>   Chief Narmer has agreed to be my
>   successor.

The crowd erupts, the leaders erupt, and everyone starts praising Narmer.

Berenib is filled with joy Narmer hugs her, and kisses her and celebrates with her first before acknowledging anyone else.

Narmer then starts acknowledging the other leaders. The entire Kustite Empire is going crazy, praising Narmer.

EXT. THE CROWNING CEREMONY AT NEKHEB - DAY

The entire Kushite Empire is present to witness the crowning ceremony. The leaders are in the front, and the people of the Empire in the crowd. Narmer and Berenib are on the stage along with the King and the Queen. The speaker begins.

>   SPEAKER
>   (beats his drum)
>   Loyal citizens of the Kushite Empire, we
>   are all gathered here today for the passing
>   of the torch. For the crowning of our new
>   King and Queen!

The crowd erupts.

>   SPEAKER
>   For years Chief Narmer has inspired us,
>   and have led us with the sole intention on
>   benefiting our Empire. Myself, nor anyone
>   else of the Empire, cannot think of anyone
>   else more deserving of this honor. As a
>   testament of our gratitude, we have
>   dedicated to our new King the city of
>   Khem. To be his capital city, and bear his
>   name! It will no longer be referred to by
>   the name Khem, but as Memphis. To
>   honor our new ruler, our new King of all
>   Kings, Narmer. So with no further delays,
>   let us all stand for the Crowning of our
>   new King of Kings Narmer and our
>   honorable Queen Berenib.

The crowd erupts, and everyone stands.

The drummers and other musicians start playing, and the people begin singing, starting the ceremony. King Salo and his Queen stand up with the crowns.

Narmer and Berenib stand up on the other side of the stage. Narmer and Berenib then walk over to the King, and Queen then kneels down in front of them. The King then puts his hand over his heart, and says a blessing to Narmer and Berenib.

The King then touches the crown on both of Narmer's shoulders. The King then puts the crown on Narmer's head. The Queen then takes her crown and touches it on both of Berenib's shoulders and then puts the crown on Berenib's head.

When both the crowns are on both Narmer's and Berenib's head they both stand up, then King Salo and his Queen both kneel down respectfully, and honors Narmer as the new King and Berenib as the new Queen.

Everyone at the ceremony also kneels down to show their respect and loyalty to the new King and Queen.

Narmer then walks up to the podium, and makes his first speech as their King. The crowd erupts. Narmer calms them down, so that he could address them.

> CHIEF NARMER
> Thank You. Thank you all. I stand here
> today in front of you honored. Honored to
> be acknowledged. Honored to be chosen,
> and honored to be your King. And to each
> and every one of you, I promise to return
> that honor. I promise to serve each and
> every one of you, by making each passing
> day more secure than the one before. I
> stand before you in Kepra, a body of
> rebirth and change. And I charge you all
> to remember this day, because today is
> the rebirth of our Empire. From this day
> forth, the Kushite Empire will never again
> be weak.

The crowd erupts and starts praising Narmer. Narmer waves, and bows to the crowd. Narmer then walks over and sits in his throne for the first time.

Berenib then walks over, and bows to the new King, then takes her seat next to Narmer. General Fusa then walks over and bows, then stands next to King Narmer.

239

All the different leaders of the Kushite Empire all line up to bow and acknowledge Narmer one at a time. They all line up to acknowledge Narmer as supreme ruler.

CREDITS ROLL.

FADE OUT.

Characters in the order they appeared

Duba: The Aswan Chief and the Aswan Warriors

Jusa: The Mumon Chief and the Momon Warriors

Jaugen:

Ben:

Alsi:

Srtife:

Fusa: General of the Nekheb Village Warriors

Narmer: Chief of the Nekheb Village

N guard 1: Narmer's personal Guard

N guard 2: Narmer's personal Guard

LAOI: Man Jaugen collect money from at the bar

Jugo: Man Jaugen collect money from at the bar

Babu: Man at the bar Jaugen tries to buy a woman from

King's Guard:

King Salo: King of the Kushite Empire

Prince Chalo: Influential member of the Royal Family

Duba: Chief of the Aswan Village

Jusa: Chief of the Mumon Village

General Masa: General of the Mumon Warriors

B Guard: Beirut Guard

Beirut: Saite Leaders at Sais the Delta region

Kalili: Saite Leaders at Sais the Delta region

Nekbeb Messengers:

Blossom: Ben's Wife

Dade: Ben's youngest Son

Ann: Ben's second Wife

Lena: Ben's Daughter

Marcus: Ben's oldest Son

Myia: Ben's second Daughter

Rose: Jaugen's Wife who is pregnant

Berenib: Narmer's Chief Wife

Djer: Narmer's oldest Son

Mnfeco: Chief of the Hierakonopolis Village

Mumba: Chief of the Semna Village

Popa: Chief of the Kerma Village

Zomi: Chief of the Kuru Village

Duka: Chief of the Kurgus Village

Rasa: Chief of the Napata Village

Srco: Chief of the Khem Village

Bobo: Chief of the Meroe Village

Gola: Chief of the Dongola Village

Speaker: Conduct the Meetings of the Council

Donoe: Leader at Athra the Delta Region

D Guard: Donoe's Guard

Meat Man: Meat Man at Buba

Sting: Leader at Buba in the Delta Region

Sais Rebels: 3 rebels at Sais

Rah: Leader at Rumah the Delta Region

Kawame: Leader at Wambe the Delta Region

S Guard 1: Sting's Guard S

1st Mem: 1 of Sting's Village Members at Buda

S 2nd Mem: 1 of Sting's Village Members at Buda

D 1st Mem: Donoe's Village Member at Athra

Z Guard: Zomi's Guard

Light Leader: Conductor of the Keepers of the Order of Light

1 Keeper: Member of the Keepers of the Order of Light

2 Keeper: Member of the Keepers of the Order of Light

3 Keeper: Member of the Keepers of the Order of Light

4 Keeper: Member of the Keepers of the Order of Light

5 Keeper: Member of the Keepers of the Order of Light

6 Keeper: Member of the Keepers of the Order of Light

7 Keeper: Member of the Keepers of the Order of Light

8 Keeper: Member of the Keepers of the Order of Light

9 Keeper: Member of the Keepers of the Order of Light

10 Keeper: Member of the Keepers of the Order of Light

11 Keeper: Member of the keepers of the Order of Light

12 Keeper: Member of the keepers of the Order of Light

Babalu Priest: At the meeting of the Keepers who works Voodoo

3rd Keeper's Guard: Informs Narmer of the landing

1st Commander: One of the landing Leaders

2nd Commander: One of the landing Leaders

General Hara: General of Thebes Village and Throne Warriors

5 Babalu Priest: At the war ceromony

Tifa: Leader of the Female Warriors

General Ourou: General of the Hierakonopolis Village Warriors

General Bungo: General of the Napata Village Warriors

General Clay: General of the Kuru Village Warriors

General Saku: General of the Meroe Village Warriors

Messenger: Carry message for Narmer during the war

Pen: The Mumon Warrior who overthrows Chief Jusa

Kem: Narmer's youngest Son

Feeze: Narmer's daughter

Shak: Narmer's next oldest Son

www.ingramcontent.com/pod-product-compliance
Lightning Source LLC
LaVergne TN
LVHW082321080426
835508LV00042B/1423